0747 804842 3505 96

Discovering

British Military Badges and Buttons

R. J. Wilkinson-Latham

D0766980

A Shire book

Contents

British Library Cataloguing in Publication Data: Wilkinson-Latham, Robert. Discovering British military badges and buttons. – 3rd ed. – (A Shire book; 148) 1. Great Britain. Army – Medals, badges, decorations etc. 2. Great Britain. Army – Insignia I. Title II. British military badges and buttons 355.1'342'0941. ISBN 0 7478 0484 2.

ACKNOWLEDGEMENTS

In the preparation of the third edition listing the recent changes and the reorganisation of the British Army, I would like to acknowledge the kind help received from the following with information, badges and illustrations: Major J. G. H. Corrigan, 6th Gurkha Rifles; Lieutenant Colonel S. J. Lindsay, The Black Watch; Major J. Hillis, MBE, The Royal Irish Regiment; Major K. A. Zambelli, Royal Armoured Corps; Colonel M. Procter, Royal Logistic Corps; Major D. W. G. Riddick, Directorate of Army Publications; and Captain A. L. Roche, Directorate of Public Relations, Ministry of Defence.

I would like to thank the following for their help with information, illustrations and badges during the writing of this book: Roy Butler of Wallis & Wallis (plates 1a, 2, 8, 9, 11, 18, 19); Brigadier T. F. J. Collins, CBE (plate 24); the Ministry of Defence (plates 20, 21 and 22a); John Gaylor, Secretary of the Military Historical Society; J. Bensusan, Curator and Archivist of the Gibraltar Museum; and T. O. Read of Dublin for photographs of head-dresses in his collection (plates 1b, 1c, 1d). Other photographs are from my own collection. The line drawings are by my wife Christine, to whom this book is dedicated, and by Jack Cassin Scott and Edward Stamp. I would also like to thank the knowledgeable members of the Salisbury Militaria Society and especially Mike Maidment for our frequent deep discussions on all things military, especially badges and buttons.

The cover photograph shows a Royal Military College gentleman cadet's shako, 1844–55. (Edward Wilkinson-Latham)

Published in 2002 by Shire Publications Ltd, Cromwell House, Church Street, Princes Risborough, Buckinghamshire HP27 9AA, UK. Website: www.shirebooks.co.uk Copyright © 1973, 1994 and 2002 by R. J. Wilkinson-Latham. First published 1973; reprinted 1986. Second edition 1994. Third edition 2002. Number 148 in the Discovering series. ISBN 0 7478 0484 2.

Printed in Great Britain by CIT Printing Services Ltd, Press Buildings, Merlins Bridge, Haverfordwest, Pembrokeshire SA61 1XF.

List of plates

1. Introduction

Distinguishing signs or marks have been used throughout history to enable friend to be recognised from foe. The Romans gave each of their legions a distinguishing sign that was painted on the shield of each soldier. Even the Saxons, who spurned 'uniform' in the sense that the Romans used it, adopted distinguishing marks on their shields. Perhaps the oldest sign that survives today is the badge of the Welsh Guards, the leek (plate 21), which was used by the Welsh as a 'field sign' as far back as AD 640.

As tactics improved and armour became more substantial, distinguishing signs became more important. Coats displaying the arms of the wearer, also borne on the shield, were worn over the armour and a crest was fitted to the top of the helmet. Each of a nobleman's soldiers bore his device on their jerkins. As wars became international, rather than between neighbouring lords, national insignia were adopted to overcome the confusion of the crests and arms of all the various noblemen fighting on the same side. In 1385 Richard II ordered every soldier of his army to wear the cross of St George emblazoned on his coat. This sign and, later, the badges of the monarch were the means by which soldiers identified their comrades and allies.

To distinguish the various regiments, colours or banners emblazoned with arms were carried. Each regiment bore a banner with the arms of its colonel on it and each company put on its flag the arms of its captain.

The regiments of Cromwell's New Model Army, formed in 1645, dressed in red with facings of various colours as distinguishing signs, but before the use of 'uniforms' and metal badges 'field signs' were used. These took many forms. The Royalists during the English Civil War used a scrap of paper in their hats, while other armies had used sprigs of laurel, acorns and leaves (the badge of The Cheshire Regiment), thistles, and roses, all of which feature in the cap badges of the British Army.

In 1751 a royal warrant was issued prohibiting personal arms being used on soldiers' clothing and regimental colours; authorised badges or numbers for each regiment were to be borne on their colours and later on their head-dress and buttons.

2. British military badges

'Badge' – an all-embracing word for a sign, symbol or device – is used in the military sense to describe an ornament worn on the uniforms, colours or accoutrements of a regiment or army to distinguish one side or one group from another. Badges were used on the colours and drums of the infantry and the standards, guidons, saddle-cloths and holster covers of the cavalry. Sabretaches (document cases slung from the waist-belt) and shabraques (saddle-cloths) were elaborately embroidered with regimental badges and battle honours, and pouches, slung in the middle of the back on a cross-belt, were often worked with the same design.

The extent of the use of badges is enormous, but this book concentrates on the metal badges worn on the head-dress and the collar of the tunic, because these, being detachable, are readily available to the collector and show many interesting variations and different patterns. The embroidered badges worn by officers on forage caps are described briefly, for they may sometimes be found. Sabretaches and shabraques, as well as colours, are not considered because the embroidery is seldom cut from the article it adorned; but undress sabretaches are included because the metal badges fitted to them may also be found separately.

Although infantry grenadiers, cavalry farriers and both cavalry and infantry drummers wore caps, it was not until 1768 that metal badges were fitted to their head-dress. Most cavalry and infantry wore hats, the former, except for Light Dragoons, until a helmet was authorised in 1812, and the latter until the introduction of the shako in 1800. Light Dragoons had in the 1760s adopted a helmet on which regimental badges were authorised to be fitted.

CAVALRY

The royal warrant of 1751 described the hats and caps of the cavalry and stated that only the Horse Grenadiers and the Royal North British Dragoons (Royal Scots Greys from 1877) were allowed to wear caps embroidered with regimental devices. The cap of the Royal North British Dragoons (fig. 1) had a blue front, a red lower flap and a red back; the turned-up band was blue with an embroidered thistle between the letters 'II' and 'D'. All Light Dragoon regiments were to wear a helmet.

The warrant also described the undress watering or forage caps, which were red with a small turned-up flap in the regimental facing colour with the number of the regiment on it. The main distinguishing badges at this period were on the drums, colours, saddle-cloths and holster covers. Cavalry drummers had the same style of embroidered cap as infantry grenadiers (plate 1a), but with the front decorated with

Fig. 1. (Left) Embroidered cap of The Royal North British Dragoons, 1751.
Fig. 2. (Right) Leather 'Tarleton' style cap of the 9th Light Dragoons, 1784.

trophies of drums and flags and with an embroidered back-band bearing a drum and the regimental number.

In 1768 a new warrant ordered farriers to wear a small bearskin cap with a metal plate showing a silver-plated horseshoe on a black background. The Royal North British Dragoons were also ordered a black bearskin cap with a plate bearing the thistle within the circle of St Andrew, inscribed with the motto '*Nemo me impune lacessit*'.

Regulations issued in 1784 for Light Dragoons ordered the cap as shown in fig. 2. The regulations stated that the distinguishing badges 'of those regiments who have any to be preserved' were to be placed on the right side of the cap. Furthermore every regiment was to have its number fitted on the front of each cap. This was normally on a band fitted above the peak (see fig. 2).

In 1796 a metal 'hot weather' helmet was introduced that had a larger plate on the front displaying the regimental number and badge.

Another item of equipment that frequently displayed the regimental badge or number was the plate that fastened the sword belt. The 1765 warrant notes that regiments of Horse and Light Dragoons wore this belt over the right shoulder, but Dragoon Guards and Dragoons had to wear it around the waist, until in 1788 they too were ordered to wear the belt across the body. The usually oval plates were silver for those regiments with silver lace and gilt for those with gold lace (for lace colours see page 31). Engraved on the face were the regimental badge and number and various honours, wreaths and foliage. Sometimes, especially with yeomanry (volunteer) cavalry, the title was placed round the edge of the plate (figs. 3 and 4).

By the early nineteenth century the cross-belt plate had been discarded and the sword was carried from a waist-belt with a buckle,

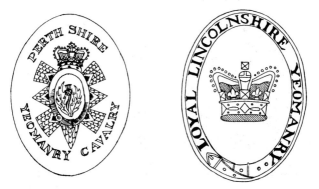

Fig. 3. (Left) Oval belt plate of the Perthshire Yeomanry Cavalry, c.1790.
Fig. 4. (Right) Oval belt plate of the Loyal Lincolnshire Yeomanry, c.1790.

which for light cavalry was usually a simple snake type with chased decoration. Dragoon Guards and Dragoons had a rectangular plate with the crowned royal cypher within a laurel wreath fitted to it. This design, but with changing cyphers, was worn by 'heavy' cavalry officers until the disappearance of full dress in 1939. Other ranks' plates bore a regimental device until the last quarter of the nineteenth century, when a snake fastening buckle was adopted.

Household Cavalry

In 1812 the Life Guards were ordered a helmet that had crests of brass and horse-hair. On the front was a plate that bore the crown over the intertwined and reversed royal cypher above an oval inscribed 'Life Guards'. This pattern was adopted by the Royal Horse Guards in about 1814 with 'Royal Horse Guards Blue' in the oval beneath the crowned cypher. In 1814 the crest was replaced by a red over blue worsted comb. In 1817 a new helmet was introduced that had the body in polished steel decorated with gilt foliage and surmounted by a bearskin crest. The front plate, which was semicircular and rayed, displayed the Hanoverian coat of arms (fig. 5), behind which, until 1820, were the Prince of Wales's feathers. Each side of the central device was a scroll bearing the words 'Peninsula' and 'Waterloo'. This pattern continued in use until 1832.

In 1820 a bearskin cap was adopted for special wear; it bore a gilt grenade on the front with the Hanoverian royal arms (fig. 5), used until 1837, raised in the centre. In 1842 the 'Albert' helmet, which had a German silver body decorated with gilt foliage and a gilt plate, was adopted. The plate displayed a cut-steel star, in the centre of which

Fig. 5. Royal coats of arms: (left) shield 1801–16; (centre) full coat of arms 1837–1901 (and after, but with a change of crown); (right) shield 1816–37.

was the Garter with motto, inside a red enamel cross on a white ground. The back plate was a crowned shield with a laurel spray on the left and an oak spray on the right (fig. 6).

In 1871 a simplified version of the helmet was introduced, with no foliage on the body, but with a cut-steel star of the same pattern. Other ranks' helmets bore a similar plate but the star was rayed and the centre was brass. This pattern is still in use today.

Fig. 6. (Left) 'Albert' cavalry helmet plate, 1848.
Fig. 7. (Right) Lance cap plate, 5th Royal Irish Lancers, 1870.

Heavy cavalry
(Except The Royal North British Dragoons, later The Royal Scots Greys)

The 1812 helmet for heavy cavalry resembled that of the Household Cavalry, with the name of the regiment on the oval plate beneath the crowned royal cypher. After 1815 regiments entitled to do so carried scrolls with the honours 'Peninsula' or 'Waterloo' or both on the plate. In 1818 a new helmet similar to the 1817 pattern of the

8

Household Cavalry, but with the body blackened instead of plain polished, was introduced. Some regiments bore honours on the plate and the 3rd and 6th bore their titles. After 1820 the Prince of Wales's feathers behind the coat of arms were omitted.

In 1834 a new all-brass pattern helmet was adopted, with a rayed plate similar in shape to that worn on lance caps. The plate carried the royal coat of arms and honours if entitled and had a band beneath with the regimental title such as '1st or King's Dragoon Guards'. In 1834 the helmet was simplified by the omission of much of the body decoration, but the plate remained the same. After 1837, however, the royal coat of arms was simplified when Victoria became queen (fig. 5).

In 1847 the 'Albert' helmet was adopted, bearing the plate shown in fig. 6 with the regimental title in the Garter. In 1871 a simplified helmet was ordered which bore on the front a twelve-pointed cut star on which was placed the Garter with the monogram 'VR' inside. Other ranks and officers of the 6th Dragoon Guards had a plain rayed plate (fig. 8). Dragoon Guard regiments had brass helmets with white metal stars and brass numerals on a black ground, while Dragoon regiments had white metal helmets, brass stars and white metal numerals on a black ground. By 1900 various regimental patterns were being worn by officers. The 2nd Dragoon Guards had the royal crest inside the Garter, the 3rd the Prince of Wales's feathers, the 4th the cross of St Patrick within a circle inscribed '*Quis separabit*' and the date 'MDCCLXXXII'. The 5th Dragoon Guards had '5' within a circle inscribed 'P.C.W. Dragoon Guards', the 6th should have had the number in the Garter but examples of this plate show the Garter inscribed 'Carabiniers'. The 1st Dragoons had the royal crest in a

Fig. 8. (Left) Other ranks' helmet plate, Dragoons and Dragoon Guards, 1871–1914.
Fig. 9. (Right) Shako plate, 4th Light Dragoons, 1855–61.

circle inscribed 'Royal Dragoons' and the 6th had the Castle of Inniskilling and 'VI' within a circle inscribed 'Inniskilling Dragoons'.

2nd Dragoons

The Royal North British Dragoons (later The Royal Scots Greys) wore a bearskin cap from 1768 until the abandonment of full dress. The late Victorian cap had a grenade on the left side that acted as a plume holder and bore on the ball the royal arms above St Andrew and his cross and the honour 'Waterloo'. On the back of the cap, often hidden by the fur, was a white metal running horse.

Light cavalry

At the beginning of the nineteenth century light cavalry divided into three distinctive groups, each with its own form of dress: Hussars (1807), Lancers (1816) and Light Dragoons. Hussar head-dress alternated between the fur busby and the shako until the busby was finally adopted in 1841. No badge was worn on the busby, distinction being by plume colour and the colour of the bag hanging on the right side. The shako worn before this bore no metal badge on the front, only lace in the form of a wheel with a regimental button in the centre.

Light Dragoons wore a shako before the light cavalry split into three parts but only the 17th appears to have had its badge, the skull and crossed bones, in metal on the front. The first Light Dragoon shako on which all regiments bore a similar metal badge was adopted in 1830. The plate was a large crowned Maltese cross adorned with a regimental badge in the circle in the centre and battle honours on the edges of the cross. This style of plate, although differing in size, was worn on the 1845–55 shako and the 1855–61 shako (fig. 9). The last Light Dragoon regiments were converted to Hussars in 1861.

The Lancers, first used in the British Army in 1816, adopted the large square-topped caps of their foreign counterparts. The front plate was similar to that of the heavy cavalry helmet; it was rayed and displayed the royal arms with regimental distinctions. The 19th Lancers (1816–21) had the honour 'Seringapatam' with an elephant beneath the royal arms; the 23rd had the sphinx and the 17th (Lancers in 1821) had the skull superimposed over crossed bones with a scroll beneath inscribed 'Or Glory'. By the 1850s the 12th had the plate shown in plate 2, while the 9th had the reversed and intertwined cypher of Queen Adelaide under a crown and over two oval shields, the left bearing the royal arms and the right the arms of Queen Adelaide (plate 2). Before 1830, when the regiment was titled 'Queen's', the plate was flat, not rayed, and had a beaded edge. In the centre there were the royal arms over a scroll inscribed 'Peninsula'.

After 1855 regiments started to include battle honours on the plate so that by the beginning of the twentieth century many plates were crammed with honours. The 16th had fourteen, the 17th had seven, the 12th had eight as well as the sphinx and 'Egypt', the 9th had sixteen, the 5th had four and the 21st only one.

The 5th (Royal Irish) Lancers were created in 1861 and bore the harp on their plate (fig. 7), while the 21st were converted from Hussars in 1897 and bore the royal arms above a scroll inscribed '21st Lancers'. In 1898 they were accorded the title 'Empress of India's' and the battle honour 'Khartoum', both of which, together with the imperial cypher 'VRI', were incorporated on the plate.

Black leather sabretaches were worn by all cavalry officers in full dress and undress, except for Hussars, who retained an elaborate embroidered version for full dress. Most of the non-embroidered sabretaches bore a metal badge on the black leather flap: the 17th Lancers, the skull and crossed bones; the 12th Lancers, the crossed lances and Prince of Wales's feathers; The Royal Scots Greys, an eagle on a tablet inscribed 'Waterloo'. Various regimental badges can be found detached, some of regular and others of yeomanry cavalry or volunteers, whose field officers wore sabretaches. The badges can be recognised by having small bolts brazed to the back. Sabretaches were discontinued in 1901.

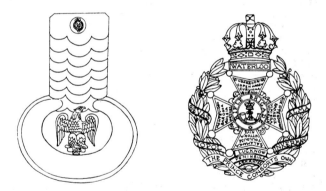

Fig. 10. (Left) Brass shoulder scales, 1st Royal Dragoons, c.1850.
Fig. 11. (Right) Cross-belt plate of The Rifle Brigade.

Cap badges

Cap badges for cavalry were not introduced until 1894, when wearing of the field service cap was authorised. Even then, the first badges worn by cavalry consisted of letters and number designating the regiment, e.g. 'VII H'. By about 1898 each regiment had adopted a proper badge for wearing on this cap. Many of the badges were the same for officers and other ranks and were later used on the peaked cap introduced in 1904. The badges were also intended to be worn on

11

the puggaree, the folded linen band on the white foreign service helmet, to distinguish the regiment.

The list below describes some variations of badge worn by the Household Cavalry and cavalry from 1900 until the Second World War.

Cap badges of cavalry regiments
Household Cavalry

Life Guards (1st and 2nd, plate 3b). In 1913 they both adopted a crowned Garter with motto with the royal cypher in the centre. For the service dress cap a crowned circle with the cypher inside was adopted but each regiment had its title in the circle, i.e. 'First Life Guards' or 'Second Life Guards'. Other ranks had worn the crowned Garter with motto and cypher inside until 1913, when they adopted the badge with regimental title for service dress, the former badge being retained for the forage cap. In 1922 the 1st and 2nd Life Guards were amalgamated, keeping the same badge but without numerical prefix.

Royal Horse Guards (plate 3b). In 1913 they adopted the same badge as the Life Guards and a similar badge for the service dress but inscribed 'Royal Horse Guards'. Other ranks adopted this pattern in 1913, retaining the crowned Garter with cypher inside for the forage cap.

Dragoon Guards

1st (plate 3b). Other ranks had a scroll beneath inscribed 'King's Dragoon Guards'. 1915, a crowned eight-pointed star with the Garter in the centre, inscribed '*Honi soit qui mal y pense*' and inside 'K' above 'D.G.', was adopted. 1937, all ranks as plate 3b.

2nd (plate 3b).

3rd (plate 3b). 1922 (amalgamated with 6th Dragoon Guards), Prince of Wales's feathers, coronet and motto superimposed on crossed carbines with scroll beneath inscribed '3rd Carabiniers' (worn after 1929).

4th (plate 4). 1922 (amalgamated with 7th Dragoon Guards), an eight-pointed star with circle in the centre inscribed '*Quis separabit*' above and 'MCMXXII' beneath. In the centre the cross of St George with the Princess Royal's coronet superimposed at its centre.

5th (plate 4). 1922 (amalgamated with 6th Dragoons), the crowned monogram 'VDG'.

6th (plate 4). 1922, amalgamated with 3rd Dragoon Guards.

7th (plate 4). 1906, brass badge in lieu of white metal, and scroll changed to one bearing motto '*Quo fata vocant*'. 1922, amalgamated with 4th Dragoon Guards.

Dragoons

1st (plate 4). 1915, the eagle with laurel wreath on the breast on a tablet inscribed '105'.

2nd (plate 4).

6th (plate 5). 1922, amalgamated with 5th Dragoon Guards.

Hussars

3rd (plate 4).

4th (plate 4). 1907, scroll added beneath inscribed '*Mente et manu*'.

7th (plate 5); **8th** (plate 5); **10th** (plate 5) and **11th** (plate 5).

13th (plate 5). The large badge was more often used on the field cap than the small one ordered. 1922 (amalgamated with 18th), crowned 'H' with 'QMO' on centre and 'XIII' above and 'XVIII' beneath. 1938, crowned monogram 'QMO' with Z-shaped scroll over inscribed 'XIII' on the top bar, 'Royal Hussars' on the diagonal and 'XVIII' on the bottom bar.

14th (plate 6). 1915, the Garter inscribed '*Honi soit qui mal y pense*' with the royal crest inside. Beneath the Garter a scroll inscribed '14th King's Hussars'. 1922 (amalgamated with 20th), scroll beneath changed to read '14th/20th Hussars'.

15th (plate 6). 1922 (amalgamated with 19th), same badge except the title joining scroll to Garter read 'XV XIX'.

18th (plate 6). 1904, crowned circle inscribed '*Pro rege, pro lege, pro patria*' with inside on a solid ground 'XVIII' over 'H', the whole encircled by an open laurel wreath. On the left branch a scroll inscribed 'Peninsula' and on the right 'Waterloo'. A scroll beneath inscribed 'Princess of Wales's'. 1905, as 1904 but bottom scroll read 'Princess of Wales's Own'. 1911, crowned circle inscribed 'Queen Mary's Own' with inside 'XVIII' superimposed on 'H'. Beneath the circle, a small spray of laurel each side. 1922, amalgamated with 13th.

19th (plate 6). 1909, elephant (with trunk curved upwards and shorter in the leg) over two scrolls, one above the other, inscribed '19th Alexandra P.W.O. Hussars'. 1922, amalgamated with 15th.

20th (plate 6). 1922, amalgamated with 14th.

Lancers

5th (plate 4). 1922, amalgamated with 16th.

9th (plate 5).

12th (plate 5). 1903, Prince of Wales's feathers, coronet and motto superimposed in the centre of crossed lances with crown between the pennons and 'XII' between the butts.

16th (plate 6). 1905, 'The' added to scroll. 1922 (amalgamated with 5th), badge remained as for 16th.

17th (plate 6). 1922 (amalgamated with 21st), badge remained as for 17th.

21st. 1898, crossed lances with crown between the pennons and 'XXI' just below the crossing. 1899, crowned monogram 'VRI' over 'XXI' between two upright lances. 1900 (plate 6). 1922, amalgamated with 17th.

In December 1940 the War Office created the 22nd Dragoons, 23rd Hussars and 24th Lancers. In 1941 the 25th Dragoons and 26th Hussars were formed as well as the 27th Lancers. The badges of these regiments were fairly simple, incorporating the crossed lances for the 24th and 27th and crossed swords for the 25th. The 26th adopted the Prussian eagle with scroll bearing the title beneath while the 22nd had a large crowned 'D' with 'XXII' inside and a scroll beneath, and the 23rd a large crowned 'H' with title in a scroll beneath. These six regiments were disbanded in 1948.

The Royal Tank Regiment, formed as the Tank Corps in July 1917 from the heavy branch of the Machine Gun Corps, had as its badge a crowned wreath with a First World War tank with gun facing right in the centre and a scroll above inscribed 'Tank' and one beneath inscribed 'Corps'. In 1922 the Corps became 'Royal' and the motto 'Fear Naught' was placed on the badge on a scroll beneath the tank in place of the two previous scrolls. In 1924 the badge was altered to make the tank face left. In 1939 the Corps became The Royal Tank Regiment.

The Royal Armoured Corps, formed in 1939, adopted the badge of a crowned laurel wreath with the monogram 'RAC' inside. In 1941 the badge was changed to that shown in fig. 39.

Arm badges

Most cavalry regiments had a distinctive arm badge that was worn by sergeants either on or above the chevrons of rank. Some of these were an enlarged version of the cap badge, but others are completely different.

INFANTRY

The 1751 warrant ordered an embroidered cap for grenadiers (plate 1a), which the warrant of 1768 replaced with a bearskin cap with a metal plate on the front and a grenade with the regimental number on the back (plate 1b). The rest of the infantry wore the cocked hat until 1800, when a shako with plate was authorised (plate 8). General Order of 24th February 1800, which introduced the shako, also prescribed that the regimental number be engraved on the plate each side of the lion. Regiments entitled to special badges were allowed them in place of the royal cypher. Grenadiers were permitted the grenade inside the Garter, if their colonels chose.

Two other items of dress on which the badge or regimental number was allowed were the cross-belt plate and the gorget. The former was oval in shape at this period but became rectangular by the early nineteenth century and gradually larger and more ornate towards 1855, when it was abolished for all except officers of Scottish regiments. The designs were all regimental, the early patterns having numbers beneath the crown, which was gradually augmented with battle honours, special mottoes and other decorative devices. Some regiments such as the The Royal Fusiliers (7th) and The King's Own Borderers (25th) adopted special ornamental patterns, while others, such as The Middlesex Regiment (57th), made use of the cut star that became popular in the 1830s. Other ranks' plates were usually a crowned numeral within an open laurel wreath, occasionally augmented with a battle honour. Other ranks' plates of the 1830–55 period were die-stamped while the earlier pattern plates were engraved.

After the disappearance of the cross-belt and plate, officers' waist-belts had special pattern regimental clasps. By 1874 other ranks had adopted a universal locket with the royal crest inside a circle inscribed '*Dieu et mon droit*', while officers were ordered to have the

14

regimental number surmounted by the crown (plate 12) in the centre and the title of the regiment in silver on the outer circle. Various regiments were allowed to have their badge as well as the number, and the 18th were allowed to have their motto in the circle and the 100th a wreath in place of the title. When the sash was ordered to be worn round the waist in 1904 the waist-belt and clasp were abolished.

Gorgets, the last relic of armour worn by the infantry officer, gradually diminished in size from the mid eighteenth century until they reached their final shape in 1829, when they disappeared. The commonest type has the crowned cypher in the centre with a spray of laurel on each side. Other examples incorporated the full coat of arms with 'G' on the left of the crown and 'R' on the right. Beneath was usually the number or title of the regiment.

Many belt plates and gorgets, especially of volunteers and local militia, bear their title in monogram and so are difficult to identify.

Returning to head-dress badges, a new pattern of shako was authorised in 1811 and taken into wear in 1812. The badge was a crowned shield of particular shape (plate 1c) with the monogram 'GR' in the centre. *Horse Guards Circular* of 14th February 1812 authorised the use of badges and numbers on the plate. The number was placed below the cypher (plate 9), while those regiments entitled to badges placed these below a slightly smaller 'GR'. In 1814 another general order stated that rifle and light infantry corps and rifle and light companies of line regiments should have, in place of the plate, a bugle horn with the number of the regiment beneath.

The so-called 'Waterloo' shako was replaced by the 'Regency' shako by General Order of 10th August 1815, coming into general use in 1816. The shako was an inverted bell shape and the regimental number, or badge and number, was displayed on a round plate surrounded by a crown and encircled in lace of regimental colour. Light infantry and light companies of line regiments bore a bugle on the shako. Other ranks' plates were in brass and bore only the regimental number.

In about 1822 the round plate was superseded by a crowned eight-pointed star on which were displayed the regimental number, badge (if entitled) and honours. In 1828 the shako was altered slightly and a universal large gilt star badge surmounted by a crown was sanctioned. Regiments took this opportunity to design some elaborate plates, some being particularly handsome, like that of the 74th (plate 3a), while others remained quite plain, like that of the 56th (plate 3a). Light companies of line regiments bore their number within the strings of a bugle on the plate (plate 3a). Other ranks' plates worn until 1839 bore the same crowned star but with a plain circle in the centre displaying the regimental number. In 1839 other ranks adopted a plate as shown in plate 10 (third row, top), with the regimental number on a lined background.

In 1844 the 'Albert' shako was adopted, with an eight-pointed star surmounted by a crown plate. Dress regulations of 1846 described the plate as follows:

> Gilt plate, a star of eight points four and a half in extreme diameter, surmounted by a crown, and bearing, within a wreath formed of laurel and palm branch, a Garter inscribed with the title of the regiment, in the centre of which is the number – the whole, including regimental badges and honorary distinctions, to be of the same metal, without any difference of colour or material.

As can be expected, many regiments interpreted these regulations in differing ways and a great variety of plates is to be found. For example, the 17th Foot had on a *circle* 'Leicestershire', with inside it a tiger over '17'. Across the base of the wreath was a scroll inscribed 'Hindoostan'. On the left central point of the star was 'Afghanistan', on the right 'Ghuznee' and on the bottom ray 'Khelat'.

The 30th had on the Garter '*Spectamur agendo*', in the centre 'XXX', beneath the wreath the sphinx over 'Egypt', on the ray to the left of the crown 'Waterloo', and on the corresponding lower ray 'Peninsula'. On the ray to the left of the crown was 'Badajoz' and on the corresponding lower ray 'Salamanca'.

The 89th had on the Garter the word 'Regiment' with inside '89'; below the wreath resting on the bottom ray was the sphinx over 'Egypt', and above the wreath was a scroll inscribed 'Niagara', on the left central ray 'Java', and on the right 'Ava'.

Regimental variations are numerous not only in the British Army but also in the armies of the Honourable East India Company and care must be taken not to confuse the two. A careful check on the battle honours displayed on the plate will aid in identification.

Fusiliers wore a large grenade plate on the shako with the regimental design on the ball. The 23rd, for example, had the Prince of Wales's feathers, coronet and motto in silver mounted on the gilt ball. The grenade measured 4³⁄₄ inches (121 mm) high.

In 1855 there was yet another type of shako, which necessitated a change in plate, the new shako not being large enough to take the old plate. The basic crowned eight-pointed star remained, but without honours on the rays, and with the regimental number on a black leather ground within the Garter with the motto, '*Honi soit qui mal y pense*' (plate 12, third row, second down). There were once again regimental variations: for example, the 18th had a circle in place of the Garter, inscribed '*Virtutis namurgensis praemium*', and in place of the plain number a crowned harp with shamrock leaves beneath. The 65th, however, retained the Garter but placed the tiger over '65' in the centre, adding above the Garter a scroll inscribed 'India' and one beneath inscribed 'Arabia'. The other ranks' plates were the same size, with the regimental number raised in the centre of the Garter. ✦

In 1861 a new shako based on the French pattern was ordered, which retained the same form of plate, though slightly reduced in size. The basic pattern worn by officers and other ranks had the regimental number pierced out of a dappled ground inside the Garter in the centre of the crowned star. Once more variations were adopted, the 52nd having the stringed bugle horn with '52' between the strings in the centre, while the 8th Foot had the running horse with '8' beneath inside the Garter with a scroll above inscribed 'King's'.

A further pattern of shako was adopted in 1869 with an entirely new design of plate. The crowned star was abandoned and replaced by a crowned Garter with motto inside an open laurel wreath with the regimental number, or badge and number, within the Garter. Other ranks bore the number only, pierced out of the dappled ground inside the Garter (plate 12). Dress regulations of 1874 detailed those regiments that were allowed to include devices on their plates:

> 1st, royal cypher and crown within the Garter of St Andrew; 2nd, lamb in silver over '2'; 3rd, dragon in gilt over '3'; 4th, lion in gilt over '4'; 6th, antelope in silver over 'VI'; 8th, white horse in silver over 'VIII'; 9th, Britannia in silver over '9'; 10th, sphinx over 'Egypt' over '10'; 14th, white horse in silver over '14' (plate 12); 17th, tiger in silver over '17'; 18th, harp and crown in silver over '18'; 27th, castle in silver over '27'; 41st, 77th and 100th, Prince of Wales's feathers, coronet and motto over the numeral; 98th, Chinese dragon in silver over '98'.

Many regiments, however, incorporated devices on their plates that were not detailed in dress regulations. The 54th fitted the sphinx over 'Marabout' on the base of the laurel wreath, and the 24th fixed the sphinx over 'Egypt' in the same place. The 100th, already accorded the badge over '100', substituted a circle inscribed 'Prince of Wales's Royal Canadian Regiment' for the Garter. The 105th did away with the Garter altogether and replaced it with a palm wreath encircling a French horn with the number '105' in the centre and a scroll on the base of the wreath inscribed '*Cede Nullis*'.

In 1878, after a couple of years of trial with selected regiments, a blue cloth helmet replaced the shako (except for depot companies, which wore it until 1881). The larger surface on the front permitted the reintroduction of the crowned star plate. Again only the authorised regiments mentioned above had their device and number in the centre in place of the number only (plate 12). In the middle of the crowned star were the Garter and motto encircled with a laurel wreath, and in the centre was the regimental number. Officers' plates were composed of two or three pieces, whereas those of the other ranks were stamped in one, with the numerals fitted on a metal bar (plate 10). Once again there were exceptions for officers. The 24th had in the centre the sphinx over 'Egypt' above 'XXIV', while the 82nd had the Prince of Wales's feathers, coronet and motto over '82'. The 105th incorporated the French horn, number and motto by leaving out the Garter, as they had previously done. The 97th had the numeral '97' in the centre but added a silver scroll at the base of the wreath inscribed '*Quo fas et gloria ducunt*', while the 44th added a sphinx over 'Egypt' beneath the Garter.

Highland regiments continued to wear the traditional feather bonnet with a regimental badge fitted to a black rosette on the left side. The 71st and 74th (from 1881 The Highland Light Infantry) continued to wear the shako with a diced band and small badge: '71' in a French horn and '74' inside the star of the Order of the Thistle. The Cameronians, The King's Royal Rifle Corps and The Rifle Brigade, who wore the helmet in 1881, changed their head-dress in the 1890s, The Cameronians to the shako similar to The Highland Light Infantry but in green, and The King's Royal Rifle Corps and Rifle Brigade to astrakhan busbies. Lowland regiments abandoned the helmet in 1904 in favour of the Kilmarnock bonnet, on which a version of the cap badge was worn.

In 1881, under the Cardwell reforms, regiments of the line from the 26th to the 109th were linked together in pairs to form single regiments of two battalions. For example, the 57th and 77th were linked to form the 1st and 2nd Battalions, The Middlesex Regiment. Each regiment, including those from 1 to 26, was given a territorial title in place of its number, and this title and the newly designed badge were worn on the helmet plates. Other ranks' plates now had a circle with the regimental title (plate 10 and fig. 12) in place of the Garter and motto, and a badge within in place of the number. Officers' plates

Fig. 12. (Left) Other ranks' infantry helmet plate, The Royal Lancaster Regiment, 1881–1901.
Fig. 13. (Right) Fusiliers' cap grenade, Royal Welsh Fusiliers, 1890.

retained the Garter but placed the regimental title on a silver scroll at the base of the laurel wreath and the new badge inside the Garter. The Essex Regiment did away with the laurel wreath and replaced it with one of oak leaves. The militia and volunteers were for the most part incorporated as the volunteer battalions of line regiments and wore the plate of their parent regiment in silver with the designation on the circle for other ranks and on an extra scroll for officers. In 1908 the Territorial Force was formed, with volunteer battalions often wearing the badge of the regular regiment but without the honours awarded to the regulars. After the South African War of 1899–1902 volunteers who had served were permitted to have the honour on their badge. One example was the 7th, 8th and 9th battalions of The Middlesex Regiment, who replaced the honour 'Albuera' with 'South Africa 1900–02'.

In the 1860s Fusiliers adopted a fur cap, on the front of which they wore a flaming grenade with the regimental number, badge and motto on the ball. Before 1881 there were five regiments of Fusiliers, the 5th, 7th, 21st, 23rd and 87th, which were increased to nine by the Cardwell reforms. Each bore a grenade with the new badge on the ball (fig. 13).

Cap badges

The first cap badge consisted of the regimental numerals worn on the pill-box cap until 1874. Officers had embroidered badges or number, while the men wore the numeral only. In 1874 the glengarry was issued for undress wear with a badge fitted to the left side. The badge took the form of a crowned Garter with the name of the regiment in it and within the number, but many regiments had designs peculiar to themselves (plates 18, 19). In 1881, when the badge was placed in the centre of the helmet plate, these centres with a crown fitted above were used on the glengarry (plate 10). In 1894, when the side cap was adopted, the glengarry badge was too large and for a few years the collar badge was worn on the cap. By 1898 special badges had been designed and issued; they were later worn on the Broderick cap (a hated peakless cap in use for two years) and the forage and service dress caps adopted in 1904. Helmet plate centres fitted with a long prong were issued to be worn fitted to the puggaree of the white foreign service helmet. When cap badges became general, these were worn on the white helmet.

Cap badges of infantry regiments (titles as at 1898)

The Royal Scots (Lothian Regiment) (1st Foot) (plate 14). Officers adopted the star of the Order of the Thistle in 1904.

The Queen's (Royal West Surrey Regiment) (2nd Foot) (plate 14). 1920, without scroll and with right front paw raised instead of left.

The Buffs (East Kent Regiment) (3rd Foot) (plate 14).

Cap badges. Fig. 14. (Left) The Princess of Wales's Own (Yorkshire Regiment), 1908. Fig. 15. (Centre) The Green Howards, 1950. Fig. 16. (Right) The Cheshire Regiment, 1922.

The King's Own (Royal Lancaster Regiment) (4th Foot) (plate 14).

The Northumberland Fusiliers (5th Foot) (plate 14). 1935, title 'Royal' granted. Badge now of two metals, the grenade in brass and the device in silver. Title in circle omitted and replaced with '*Quo fata vocant*'.

The Royal Warwickshire Regiment (6th Foot) (plate 14).

The Royal Fusiliers (City of London Regiment) (7th Foot) (plate 14). In 1901 the crown was placed on the neck of the grenade.

The King's (Liverpool Regiment) (8th Foot) (plate 14). 1926, horse made larger and scroll bore 'King's' in place of 'The King's'.

The Norfolk Regiment (9th Foot) (plate 14 – officers 1900). Other ranks had Britannia within a wreath on a scroll inscribed 'The Norfolk Regt'. 1937, badge changed to a plain Britannia.

The Lincolnshire Regiment (10th Foot) (plate 13). 1946, title 'Royal' granted. 'Egypt' on tablet changed to Roman letters and 'Royal Lincolnshire Regiment' on scroll.

The Devonshire Regiment (11th Foot) (plate 13).

The Suffolk Regiment (12th Foot) (plate 13). There are versions with a two-turreted castle worn before 1900 and reintroduced sometime during the first decade of the twentieth century.

The Prince Albert's (Somerset Light Infantry) (13th Foot) (plate 13).

The Prince of Wales's Own (West Yorkshire Regiment) (14th Foot) (plate 13).

The East Yorkshire Regiment (15th Foot) (plate 13).

The Bedfordshire Regiment (16th Foot) (plate 13). 1919, star cut not rayed and scroll with title placed beneath and altered to 'The Bedfordshire and Hertfordshire Regiment'.

The Leicestershire Regiment (17th Foot) (plate 13). 1946, title 'Royal' granted and placed on scroll.

The Royal Irish Regiment (18th Foot) (plate 13). 1922, disbanded.

The Princess of Wales's Own (Yorkshire Regiment) (19th Foot) (plate 7). 1896–1908 (fig. 14). 1908 onwards (fig. 15).

The Lancashire Fusiliers (20th Foot) (plate 7).

The Royal Scots Fusiliers (21st Foot) (plate 7).

The Cheshire Regiment (22nd Foot) (plate 7). 1922 (fig. 16).

The Royal Welsh Fusiliers (23rd Foot) (plate 7). 1920, 'Welsh' changed to 'Welch'.

Cap badges. Fig. 17. (Left) The Gloucestershire Regiment. Fig. 18. (Centre) The Worcestershire Regiment, 1925. Fig. 19. (Right) The East Lancashire Regiment.

The South Wales Borderers (24th Foot) (plates 7 and 10).

The King's Own Scottish Borderers (25th Foot) (plate 7).

The Cameronians (Scottish Rifles) (26th/90th) (plate 7).

The Royal Inniskilling Fusiliers (27th/108th). A brass grenade with on the ball the Castle of Inniskilling with flag of St George blowing to the left (when viewed) above a scroll inscribed 'Inniskilling'. 1926, grenade discarded and the castle with scroll above worn. 1934, grenade badge readopted but with flag blowing to the right.

The Gloucestershire Regiment (28th/61st) (fig. 17). A 'back badge' of a sphinx over a tablet inscribed 'Egypt'; the whole in a laurel wreath was worn on the back of the cap. Prior to 1881, a back number was worn on the helmet and shako.

The Worcestershire Regiment (29th/36th). Up to 1925, on an eight-pointed star, the Garter and motto with the lion of England inside. Beneath the Garter a scroll inscribed 'Firm' and beneath the star a scroll inscribed 'Worcestershire'. 1925 (fig. 18).

The East Lancashire Regiment (30th/59th) (fig. 19).

The East Surrey Regiment (31st/70th) (fig. 20).

The Duke of Cornwall's Light Infantry (32nd/46th) (fig. 21).

The Duke of Wellington's (West Riding Regiment) (33rd/76th) (fig. 22).

Cap badges. Fig. 20. (Left) The East Surrey Regiment. Fig. 21. (Centre) The Duke of Cornwall's Light Infantry. Fig. 22. (Right) The Duke of Wellington's (West Riding Regiment).

Cap badges. Fig. 23. (Left) The Border Regiment. Fig. 24. (Centre) The Sherwood Foresters (Notts and Derby), 1902. Fig. 25. (Right) The Loyal North Lancashire Regiment, 1920.

The Border Regiment (34th/55th) (fig. 23).

The Royal Sussex Regiment (35th/107th) (plate 15).

The Hampshire Regiment (37th/67th) (plate 15). 1946, title 'Royal' granted and added to scroll.

The South Staffordshire Regiment (38th/80th) (plate 15).

The Dorsetshire Regiment (39th/54th) (plate 15). 1951, title changed to 'Dorset' Regiment and placed on the scroll.

The Prince of Wales's Volunteers (South Lancashire Regiment) (40th/82nd) (plate 15).

The Welsh Regiment (41st/69th) (plate 15). 1920, 'Welsh' changed to 'Welch'.

The Black Watch (Royal Highlanders) (42nd/73rd) (plate 15). 1934, title scrolls omitted.

The Oxfordshire Light Infantry (43rd/52nd) (plate 15). Title changed to Oxfordshire and Buckinghamshire Light Infantry in 1908, but no badge change.

The Essex Regiment (44th/56th) (plate 15).

The Sherwood Foresters (Derbyshire Regiment) (45th/95th). 1902 (fig. 24). 1900–2, scroll beneath read only 'Derbyshire'. 1903 onward (fig. 24).

The Loyal North Lancashire Regiment (47th/81st). 1920 (fig. 25). 1900–20, the scroll read 'Loyal North Lancashire'.

Cap badges. Fig. 26. (Left) The Northamptonshire Regiment. Fig. 27. (Centre) Princess Charlotte of Wales's (Royal Berkshire Regiment). Fig. 28. (Right) The Queen's Own Royal West Kent Regiment.

The Northamptonshire Regiment (48th/58th) (fig. 26).

Princess Charlotte of Wales's (Royal Berkshire Regiment) (49th/66th) (fig. 27).

The Queen's Own Royal West Kent Regiment (50th/97th) (fig. 28).

The King's Own (Yorkshire Light Infantry) (51st/105th) (fig. 29).

The King's Shropshire Light Infantry (53rd/85th) (fig. 30).

The Duke of Cambridge's Own (Middlesex Regiment) (57th/77th) (plate 10).

The King's Royal Rifle Corps (60th). A blacked Maltese cross with crowned tablet above inscribed '*Celer et audax*' with in the centre a circle inscribed 'The King's' above and 'Royal Rifle Corps' beneath. Within the circle, a stringed bugle horn. Each arm of the cross bore regimental battle honours. When worn, a red cloth patch was placed behind the badge.

The Duke of Edinburgh's (Wiltshire Regiment) (62nd/99th) (plate 16). 1954, when the present Duke of Edinburgh became Colonel-in-Chief, the monogram in the centre changed from 'A.E.A.' to reversed and intertwined 'P' with coronet above.

The Manchester Regiment (63rd/96th) (plate 16). 1923, a fleur-de-lys adopted in place of the arms of the city.

The Prince of Wales's (North Staffordshire Regiment) (64th/98th) (plate 16).

The York and Lancaster Regiment (65th/84th) (plate 16).

The Durham Light Infantry (68th/106th) (plate 16).

The Highland Light Infantry (71st/74th) (plate 16).

The Seaforth Highlanders (Ross-shire Buffs, The Duke of Albany's) (72nd/78th) (plate 16 for officers; other ranks without coronet and initial).

The Gordon Highlanders (75th/92nd) (plate 16).

The Queen's Own Cameron Highlanders (79th) (plate 16).

The Royal Irish Rifles (83rd/86th) (plate 17). 1913, white metal instead of blackened.

Princess Victoria's (Royal Irish Fusiliers) (87th/89th) (plate 17).

The Connaught Rangers (88th/94th) (plate 17). 1922, disbanded.

The Princess Louise's (Argyll and Sutherland Highlanders) (91st/93rd) (plate 17).

The Prince of Wales's Leinster Regiment (Royal Canadians) (100th/109th) (plate 17). 1922, disbanded,

Cap badges. Fig. 29. The King's Own Yorkshire Light Infantry. Fig. 30. The King's Shropshire Light Infantry.

The Royal Munster Fusiliers (101st/104th) (plate 17). 1922, disbanded.
The Royal Dublin Fusiliers (102nd/103rd) (plate 17). 1922, disbanded.
The Rifle Brigade (The Prince Consort's Own) (1803–16, 95th or Rifle
    Regiment) (plate 17) (fig. 11). 1903, without Gwelphic crown. 1910, ten
    more honours added to wreath. 1937, 'The' added to title in centre; First
    World War honours in place of 'Peninsula' at the base and extra scroll added
    at base of wreath inscribed 'Prince Consort's Own'.

During the Second World War a number of infantry and corps
badges were manufactured in plastic and issued to the troops. Two
examples are shown in plate 10. Three differing colours were used,
grey, caramel and dark brown. Smaller versions of the cap badge were
produced after the Second World War for wear on the beret.

ARTILLERY AND CORPS
Artillery

Before the introduction of the shako in 1800 for Foot Artillery and
the helmet in 1793 for the Horse Artillery, there were no badges worn
on the full-dress head-dress. In 1779 permission had been granted to
a number of Foot Artillery battalions to wear shoulder-belt plates and
by 1796 the Master General of the Ordnance complied with the
various demands he had received and ordered a cross-belt plate in the
same style as the infantry. The early plates were oval and bore the title
'Royal Artillery' and the crowned Garter on a star with 'GR' inside.
About 1790 the other ranks' plates bore the shield of the Ordnance
arms with the words 'Royal Artillery'. Illustrated (plate 12) is an
example of an other ranks' plate with the word 'British' added. This
is thought to be in order to differentiate between British and Irish
artillery, which were two separate bodies until merged in 1801. The
later belt plate, c.1823, had the crowned Garter over thunderbolts. In
1833 this was superseded by the plate illustrated in fig. 31, which,
however, shows the plate after 1837 with Victorian and not
Hanoverian arms. This plate was worn by both officers and other
ranks until it was abolished in favour of a waist-belt and plate in April
1849. The Horse Artillery wore a snake clasp on the waist-belt and
this was also worn by the Foot Artillery from 1855 as a full-dress
plate. In undress the plate was rectangular with the coat of arms over
'*Ubique*'.

The shako plate adopted in 1800 by the Foot Artillery was similar
to that of the infantry (plate 8), except that in the Garter were the
words 'Royal Regt. of Artillery' and beneath the Garter was a mortar
on its bed with a pile of shot each side. In 1812 this was superseded
by the plate shown in plate 8, which gave way to a new pattern in
about 1816. The new plate had a crowned Garter inscribed as the 1800
plate with the reversed and intertwined cypher within. This was
mounted on a circular plate with a roped edge. By 1828 the plate was

Fig. 31. (Left) Cross-belt plate, Royal Artillery, 1833–49.
Fig. 32. (Right) Light Dragoon style cap plate, Royal Horse Artillery, 1800.

that shown in plate 12, which was retained for other ranks until 1846. In 1839 officers adopted a crowned cut star with the field gun above a scroll inscribed '*Ubique*'. In 1846 both officers and other ranks adopted the plate shown in plate 10.

In 1855 the Royal Artillery adopted the busby with a grenade plume holder on the left side. This style was also used by volunteer artillery and militia artillery until 1878, when the helmet with plate as shown in plate 10 was authorised for both regular, militia and volunteer artillery. In 1928 the busby was again authorised for officers only, full dress having been abolished for other ranks at the end of the First World War.

The Royal Horse Artillery retained the Light Dragoon pattern helmet until 1828, with a variety of badges. The other ranks' plate was a crowned circle displaying three guns, one above the other, while the officers had a crowned Garter inscribed 'Royal Horse Artillery' with the reversed and intertwined cypher 'GR' inside (fig. 32). By 1855 the Royal Horse Artillery had adopted a busby without badge, which they continued to wear until the abolition of full dress, although The King's Troop, Royal Horse Artillery, still retains the busby as ceremonial head-dress today.

The cap badge of the Artillery, the crowned field gun with scroll above the gun inscribed '*Ubique*' and one beneath inscribed '*Quo fas et gloria ducunt*', was adopted for the service cap in 1902, brass for the other ranks and bronzed for officers, who also had a gilt version for the forage cap. The Royal Horse Artillery also wore this badge but had a special one produced for wear on the white helmet. In 1948 this was adopted officially for the Royal Horse Artillery in place of the field gun badge.

Between 1916 and 1918 the badge appeared with the space between the spokes of the wheel not pierced, as an economy measure. Officer badges have the distinction of an extra pinned-on wheel. There are varieties of the cap badge, some having the '*Ubique*' scroll replaced by one with laurel sprays, which was for Territorials, others with the word 'Volunteers', and others which had the title in the scroll, such as the West Riding Royal Horse Artillery, which bore 'West Riding' in place of '*Ubique*'.

Canadian, New Zealand and other Commonwealth artillery retained the same badge but with modifications on the top scroll. For example, Canada replaced '*Ubique*' with the name of the dominion. The Honourable Artillery Company also uses the field gun badge for its artillery battery but without the Royal Artillery honour and motto. In their place they have on the top scroll 'HAC' and on the bottom '*Arma pacis fulcra*'.

Corps of Royal Engineers

The Royal Engineers have retained the same style of badge from 1900 until the present day. This consisted of the Victorian pattern of a crowned Garter inscribed 'Royal Engineers', with 'VR' inside, on an open laurel wreath. In 1901 this pattern was changed to incorporate 'ER VII' within a crowned Garter with motto, and the title was placed on a scroll beneath the Garter. On the full-dress head-dress, the busby until 1878, they bore a grenade with the royal arms and '*Quo fas et gloria ducunt*'. On the helmet, this badge was enlarged and placed on the front. The pouch badge, which was the same design as the helmet plate, was smaller.

Royal Corps of Transport

Before 1965, when they were the Royal Army Service Corps, the badge was a crowned Garter with motto, with the royal cypher within a scroll beneath, resting on the base of the encircling laurel wreath inscribed 'Royal Army Service Corps', the whole superimposed on an eight-pointed star. Prior to 1918, when they were accorded the prefix 'Royal', the monogram 'ASC' took the place of the cypher and there was no scroll. The Royal Corps of Transport was formed in 1965 and had the same badge as its predecessor, the Royal Army Service Corps, but with the new title on the scroll at the base of the badge.

Royal Army Ordnance Corps

Until 1919, when they were accorded the prefix 'Royal', the corps badge bore the shield of the Ordnance arms with scroll beneath, inscribed 'Army Ordnance Corps'. In 1919 the shield was placed with the crowned Garter with scroll beneath, inscribed 'Royal Army

Ordnance Corps'. In 1947 the badge was made smaller and the scroll read '*Sua tela tonnanti*'.

Royal Corps of Signals (plate 20)

The Royal Corps of Signals was formed in 1920 from the Signals section of the Royal Engineers. The badge was an oval band surmounted by a crown, the band inscribed with 'Royal Corps of Signals' in brass with winged Mercury on a globe in white metal in the centre. In 1947 the Corps adopted a simpler badge of a brass crown (separate) over winged Mercury on a globe (in white metal) with a three-part scroll (in brass) behind with motto.

Royal Army Medical Corps (plate 21 and fig. 57)

In June 1898 officers and warrant officers of the Medical Staff Corps were merged with other ranks to form the Royal Army Medical Corps. The badge adopted was, and still is, a crowned laurel wreath with, in the centre, the rod of Aesculapius with a serpent entwined around it. A scroll beneath the whole reads 'Royal Army Medical Corps'. The only changes in design since 1898 have been to the style of the crown.

Corps of Royal Electrical and Mechanical Engineers (plate 21 and fig. 56)

The first badge of the Corps, which was formed in 1942, was an oval crowned laurel wreath with four small shields at the compass points. The top shield under the crown bore an R, with the shields on the central left and right bearing the letters E and M respectively. The shield at the centre bottom bore the letter E, the four spelling out 'REME'. In 1947 the corps received a new badge of a crown over a scroll bearing 'R.E.M.E.' with a lightning flash beneath, all in brass, with a horse with roped neck collar standing on a globe in white metal superimposed.

Royal Military Police (plate 21)

Until February 1926 the Military Police were divided into the Military Mounted Police and the Military Foot Police. The badge was the royal cypher surmounted by a crown within a laurel wreath. Below was a scroll inscribed 'Military Police'. The prefix 'Royal' was accorded in 1946.

Royal Army Pay Corps

Like other corps, the predecessors of the Royal Army Pay Corps were made up of one corps for officers and one department or corps for other ranks. The Army Pay Corps was formed in 1893 and consisted of other ranks; it was granted the prefix 'Royal' in 1920. Officers were formed into the Army Pay Department in 1878, with a title change to Army Accounts Department in 1905. In 1909 the name reverted to Army Pay Department and in 1920 the prefix 'Royal' was granted. In the same year they amalgamated with the Royal Army Pay Corps to form the Royal Army Pay Corps. The badge was 'RAPC' in script surmounted by the royal crest. In 1929 the badge was altered to the royal crest with scroll beneath, with the words '*Fide et fiducia*'.

Royal Army Veterinary Corps (plate 22a)

The Army Veterinary Department was formed in 1881, when all cavalry veterinary officers, except the Household Cavalry, were transferred to the new corps. In 1903 the Army Veterinary Corps was formed, consisting of NCOs and men. In 1906 it was amalgamated with the Army Veterinary Department to form the Army Veterinary Corps. The badge was a crowned laurel wreath with the initials AVC superimposed and intertwined in the centre. In 1918 it was granted the prefix 'Royal' and adopted a new badge of a crowned laurel wreath with a centaur in the centre and a scroll beneath with the title 'Royal Army Veterinary Corps'. With change to the crown, this badge is still worn today.

Small Arms School Corps (plate 22a)

The corps had it beginnings with the School of Musketry formed in 1854 and changed its designation to 'Small Arms School Hythe' in 1919. In 1926 it was amalgamated with the Machine Gun School at Netheravon and in 1929 they became the Small Arms School Corps. The badge of the corps is a closed wreath with a three-part scroll laid on it, bearing the title 'Small Arms School', with in the centre a crown over a Vickers machine-gun with two crossed Short Magazine Lee Enfield rifles superimposed.

Military Provost Staff Corps (plate 21)

The Military Prison Staff Corps was formed in 1901 and redesignated the 'Military Provost Staff Corps' in 1906. Its badge was the crowned royal cypher. The corps is now part of the Adjutant General's Corps (Provost Branch, MPS) and wears the badge of the crowned royal cypher with title scroll beneath.

Royal Army Educational Corps

The Army Educational Corps was formed in 1920 and made up from personnel of the disbanded Corps of Army Schoolmasters, which had been formed in 1846. The cap badge was an open book superimposed on crossed rifles and lances with a three-part scroll with title. In 1946 it was granted the prefix 'Royal' and adopted a new badge of the crown over a scroll with 'R.A.E.C', both superimposed on a flaming torch.

28

Royal Army Dental Corps (plate 22a)

The corps was formed in 1921 with a badge consisting of a crowned laurel wreath with the initials 'ADC' superimposed and intertwined in the centre. On being granted the prefix 'Royal' in 1946, the corps adopted its present-day badge of a crowned laurel wreath with three-part scroll superimposed on the lower part with the motto '*Ex dentibus ensis*' with a dragon with a sword in its teeth in the centre.

Intelligence Corps (plate 22a)

Formed in 1940, the Intelligence Corps badge is a crowned Tudor rose flanked by laurels over a scroll with the title 'Intelligence Corps'. Until 1956 the badge was brass but after that date white metal was used.

Army Physical Training Corps (plate 22a)

The original Army Physical Training Staff was formed in 1860, becoming the Army Physical Training Corps in 1940. Its badge, then as now, is a crown over crossed curved-bladed swords.

General Service Corps (plate 22a)

The General Service Corps badge is the royal arms. In 1914 the General List was for officers who had been gazetted and officers 'who are holding other appointments'.

3. British military buttons

Before 1767 buttons in the British Army bore no regimental design or identification, although some officers' buttons may have had a simple motif on them. In 1751 the infantry and the bulk of the cavalry were numbered in order of precedence, the infantry from 1 to 70, and the cavalry, excluding the Household Cavalry and Dragoon Guards, from 1st to 13th Dragoons.

After numbering in 1751, infantry regiments became known as, for example, 'The 10th Regiment of Foot' and not by the name of the colonel, as was the previous practice. Royal regiments were called, for example, 'The 2nd (Queen's Royal) Regiment of Foot', instead of 'The Queen's Own Regiment of Foot', the title used since 1727.

For the cavalry it was a little more complicated, as the Household Cavalry and the regiments of horse that later became Dragoon Guards had been numbered in the 1680s, but regiments of Dragoons, which had gone under the name of their colonel before 1751, were then numbered from 1st to 13th Dragoons; the 14th were not numbered until 1776. The War Office order of 21st September 1767 directed that numbered buttons would be fitted at the next supply of clothing for the rank and file, and for officers when they purchased new ones. This order also extended to the Dragoon Guards, who, although previously known by numbers, presumably did not bear them on their buttons.

CAVALRY

Immediately the new order came out the Dragoon Guards objected, and in December 1767 it was decided that the three regiments should be allowed to have their initials on the buttons in place of the numbers. The 1st, 2nd and 3rd Irish Horse, in 1788 the 4th Royal Irish Regiment of Dragoon Guards, the 5th Dragoon Guards and the 6th Dragoon Guards (Carabiniers) had numbered buttons. The order was not immediately carried out as some of the regiments were not yet due for clothing or were abroad, but generally by the 1770s every regiment had its own design of button. The exact date of adoption can be gleaned from inspection reports, which note whether buttons were yet numbered or not. For example, the 3rd Horse (later 6th Dragoon Guards Carabiniers) did not receive numbered buttons until 1771, while the 1st Horse (later 4th Royal Irish Dragoon Guards) received theirs in 1769.

The exact designs used on these early buttons are difficult to determine as they were rarely recorded and, if they were, the description was often ambiguous. We can, however, identify buttons by surviving examples, but these alas are few.

As a rule the buttons worn in the cavalry depended on the colour of lace that adorned the uniform coat – silver lace with silver buttons, or gold lace with gilt buttons. Other ranks' buttons corresponded to the colour worn by the officers – white lace, white metal buttons; or yellow lace, brass buttons.

Officers' buttons usually had the gilt or silver face of the button mounted on a bone or wooden backing, to which strands of gut were attached for fastening to the coat. The other ranks' buttons were also made like this, but during the last quarter of the eighteenth century these types gave way to an all-metal button with the face turned over an inner disc to which was fitted a metal shank like that used on the pewter buttons of the other ranks in the infantry.

In 1768 a Royal Clothing Warrant was issued in which the various button and lace colours were designated. Regiments with 'yellow' or brass buttons were: Dragoon Guards – 1, 2, 3; Horse – 2, 4; Dragoons – 1, 3, 13. Regiments with 'white' or white metal buttons were: Horse – 1, 3; Dragoons – 2, 4, 5, 6, 7, 8, 9, 10, 11, 14; Light Dragoons – 12, 15, 16, 17, 18.

In 1788 the four regiments of Horse were converted to Dragoon Guards and numbered 4 to 7, with the 4th, 5th and 6th having white buttons and the 7th yellow. Before and after this some Dragoon regiments were converted to Light Dragoons: 7th (1784), 8th (1777), 9th (1783), 10th (1783), 11th (1783), 13th (1783) and 14th (1776).

The buttons were either incised or stamped with the approved number or design and those regiments that had a special device or badge that was reflected in their title, i.e. the 6th or Inniskilling Dragoons, started to incorporate this design, at least in part, on their buttons. This cannot, however, be accepted as a general rule. The 3rd Regiment of Dragoon Guards was renamed the 3rd Regiment (Prince of Wales's) Dragoon Guards in 1765 but was noted in the 1769 inspection report as having gold numbered buttons. The well-known motif of the Prince of Wales's feathers was not incorporated on the buttons until the nineteenth century.

By 1800 a number of regiments had their special badges on their buttons, but these are difficult to date as some regiments changed their button designs with remarkable frequency. For example, the 8th (King's Royal Irish) Light Dragoons, who were noted as having silver numbered buttons in 1768, by 1784 had a button incised with a lion, harp and crown and regimental number, but by the early nineteenth century they had reverted to a silver button with the Roman numeral 'VIII' with 'L' above and 'D' beneath.

Certain regiments with some frequency changed not only the design of their buttons but also the colour of their lace and buttons. A certain number of Light Dragoon regiments were permitted to dress themselves as 'Hussars' after the continental fashion: the 7th (Queen's Own) Light Dragoons Hussars (1807), the 10th or Prince of Wales's Own Hussars (1806), the 15th (or the King's) Light Dragoons (Hussars) (1807) and the 18th King's (1807). These regiments in

Fig. 33. Buttons (from left to right): 17th Lancers, 1822–55; 5th Royal Irish Dragoons, 1767–99; 4th Light Dragoons, c.1830; 3rd Dragoons, 1761 to c.1800.

consequence adopted ball buttons in silver with various designs: the 7th with incised '7 LD'; the 10th with 'XH' and the Prince of Wales's coronet and feathers; the 15th with incised 'KLD 15'; and the 18th with a leaf design around the outer edge and the incised '18 LD'.

The King's Dragoon Guards had a flat button with the Garter and motto on a rayed star surmounted by a crown with the letters 'KDG'. The 2nd had a domed button with a rayed star with a circle in the centre bearing 'Q's DG'. The 3rd had adopted the Prince of Wales's coronet, motto and feathers with the letters 'D.G.'. The outer edge of the domed button was decorated with the Garter and motto.

By 1812 the following regiments had yellow buttons: Dragoon Guards – 1, 3, 5, 7; Dragoons – 1, 2, 3; Light Dragoons – 8, 9, 13, 19, 20, 22, 24, 25. The Hussars are mentioned above. In 1814, however, the 7th Hussars changed their buttons and lace from silver to gold.

In 1816 the 9th, 12th, 16th, 19th and 23rd Light Dragoons were dressed and equipped as Lancers, again following the continental fashion. Each regiment retained its previous button colour except for the 12th, which switched to yellow. From surviving buttons, it appears that only the 16th incorporated the crossed-lance design on their buttons at this early period, the 9th adopting theirs about 1835, and the 12th about 1840. Both the 19th and the 23rd were disbanded in 1821. In their place the 17th Light Dragoons were made Lancers, retaining silver lace and adopting the button shown in fig. 33.

It is not possible to describe or illustrate all the various designs, for many of them are unknown. Even in 1822, with the advent of dress regulation that laid down officers' dress, buttons when described are noted as being 'of regimental pattern'. In 1830, when William IV became king, his far-reaching reforms of the services had an immediate effect. In future all regular regiments would wear only gold lace, silver being used by the militia and certain yeomanry regiments only. This order affected the cavalry more than the infantry, because of the number of buttons and the amount of lace adorning the elaborate Hussar jackets. The other ranks reverted to yellow buttons, but it was some time before the white or pewter buttons were laid aside. Some regiments were now adopting button designs that they were to retain with only small modifications until the end of the century. The 5th Princess Charlotte of Wales's Dragoon Guards had the letters 'VDG' in relief on a ribbed ground surrounded by a Garter with the motto '*Vestigia nulla retrorsum*' on a sunken rayed star. When

Plate 1a (above left). Mitre cap, 1751. Plate 1b (above right). Grenadier cap, 97th Foot, c.1790 (front). Plate 1c (below left). Infantry officer's shako, 1812–16. Plate 1d (below right). Troop sergeant-major's lance cap, 17th, c.1850.

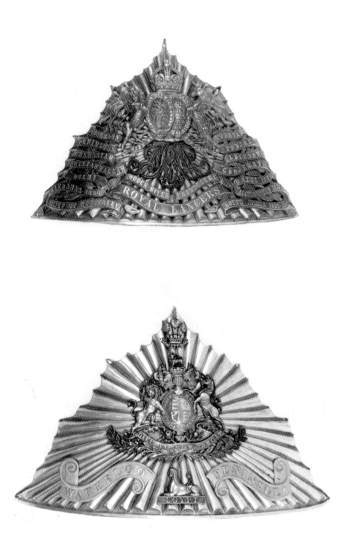

Plate 2. (Top) Officer's lance cap plate, 9th, c.1910. (Bottom) Officer's lance cap plate, 12th, c.1840.

Plate 3a. Shako plates: (left) Light Company, 80th, c.1835; (centre) 74th Foot, c.1835; (right) 56th Foot, c.1835.

Plate 3b. Cap badges, 1900: (top row, left to right) 2nd Life Guards, 1st Life Guards, Royal Horse Guards; (bottom row, left to right) 1st (King's) Dragoon Guards, 2nd Dragoon Guards (Queen's Bays), 3rd (Prince of Wales's) Dragoon Guards.

Plate 4. Cap badges, 1900: (top row, left to right) 4th (Royal Irish) Dragoon Guards, 5th (Princess Charlotte of Wales's) Dragoon Guards, 6th Dragoon Guards (Carabiniers); (centre row) 7th (Princess Royal's) Dragoon Guards, 1st (Royal) Dragoons, 2nd Dragoons (Royal Scots Greys); (bottom row) 3rd (King's Own) Hussars, 4th (Queen's Own) Hussars, 5th (Royal Irish) Lancers (puggaree badge).

Plate 5. Cap badges, 1900: (top row, left to right) 6th (Inniskilling) Dragoons, 7th (Queen's Own) Hussars (puggaree and field cap badges), 8th (King's Royal Irish) Hussars; (centre row) 9th (Queen's Royal) Lancers, 10th (Prince of Wales's Own) Royal Hussars, 11th (Prince Albert's Own) Hussars; (bottom row) 12th (Prince of Wales's) Royal Lancers, 13th Hussars (puggaree and field cap badges).

Plate 6. Cap badges, 1900: (top row, left to right) 14th (King's) Hussars (puggaree and field cap badges), 15th (King's) Hussars; (centre row) 16th (Queen's) Lancers, 17th (Duke of Cambridge's Own) Lancers, 18th Hussars; (bottom row) 19th (Prince of Wales's Own) Hussars, 20th Hussars, 21st (Empress of India's) Lancers.

Plate 7. Cap badges, 1900: (top row, left to right) The Princess of Wales's Own (Yorkshire Regiment), The Lancashire Fusiliers, The Royal Scots Fusiliers; (centre row) The King's Own Scottish Borderers, The Cheshire Regiment, The South Wales Borderers; (bottom row) The Royal Welsh Fusiliers, The Cameronians (Scottish Rifles) (puggaree and glengarry badges).

Plate 8. (Top row, left to right) Infantry shako plate 1800–12; sabretache badge of The London and Westminster Light Horse Volunteers, c.1810; other ranks' cross-belt plate, 92nd, c.1800; cross-belt plate, possibly Ashford Artillery, c.1800; glengarry badge, 21st Royal North British Fusiliers, pre-1881. (Second row) Officer's helmet plate, The Lothian Regiment, worn May to July 1881; officer's helmet plate, The Royal Scots, July 1881 to 1904; officer's helmet plate, The West India Regiment, 1881. (Bottom row) Officer's shako plate, Royal Artillery, 1812–16; other ranks' shako plate, Royal Artillery, 1812–16; shako plate, Scottish Borderers Militia, 1855–61.

Plate 9. (Top row, left to right) Shako plate, 21st Foot, 1812–16; shako plate, 57th Foot 1812–16; shako plate, 51st Foot, 1844–55. (Second row) Officer's cross-belt plate, The King's Own Scottish Borderers, 1901–53; officer's cross-belt plate, 23rd Foot, 1840–55; officer's cross-belt plate, 18th Bombay Native Infantry, c.1850. (Bottom row) Officer's shako plate, 5th Bengal European Regiment, 1844–55; cross-belt plate, The Prince of Wales's Loyal Volunteers, c.1800; officer's shako plate, 41st Foot, 1844–55.

Plate 10. *(From left, first vertical row, top to bottom) Other ranks' helmet plate, 24th Foot, 1878–81; other ranks' helmet plate centre, The Middlesex Regiment, 1881–1914; other ranks' helmet plate centre as glengarry badge, 1881–94. (Second row) Plastic cap badge, The South Wales Borderers, 1941; plastic cap badge, The Middlesex Regiment, 1941; cap badge, The South Wales Borderers, 1894–1958; anodised cap badge (Staybright), The Royal Irish Rangers, 1968. (Third row) Other ranks' shako plate, Royal Jersey Militia, 1839–55 pattern – regular regiments having their numeral in the centre; helmet plate, 3rd Middlesex Rifle Volunteers, 1881; waist-belt clasp, 1st Volunteer Battalion The Royal Lancaster Regiment. (Fourth row) Shoulder title, The South Wales Borderers; collar badge, 21st Lancers; martingale ornament, The Royal Dragoons; glengarry badge, pre-1881, 24th Foot. (Fifth row) Other ranks' shako plate, Royal Artillery, 1846–55; officer's helmet plate, Royal Artillery, 1878–1928; shoulder title, The Brecknockshire Regiment (Territorial Army). Note that shortened regimental titles are given for reference.*

Plate 11. Officer's Waterloo shako plate, 76th Foot; officer's Waterloo shako plate, 33rd Foot (later 1st and 2nd Battalions The Duke of Wellington's Regiment); other ranks' cross-belt plate; officer's cross-belt plate.

Plate 12. (Left-hand row, top to bottom) Other ranks' shako plate, 24th Foot, 1869–78; officer's forage cap badge, 1881–1904; officer's waist-belt clasp, 24th Foot, 1874–81; cross-belt plate, Royal British Artillery, c.1800. (Middle row) Officer's helmet plate, 57th Foot, 1878–81; shako plate, Royal Artillery, c.1830; metal helmet badge, Derbyshire Yeomanry, 1871–1900. (Right-hand row) Officer's shako plate, 14th Foot, 1869–78 (crown missing); officer's shako plate, 24th Foot, 1855–61 (crown missing); waist-belt clasp, Control Department, 1865–75; general officer's martingale ornament showing Gwelphic crown, c.1890.

Plate 13. Cap badges, 1900: (top row, left to right) The Lincolnshire Regiment, The Devonshire Regiment, The Suffolk Regiment; (centre row) The Prince Albert's (Somerset Light Infantry), The Prince of Wales's Own (West Yorkshire Regiment), The East Yorkshire Regiment; (bottom row) The Bedfordshire Regiment, The Leicestershire Regiment, The Royal Irish Regiment.

Plate 14. Cap badges, 1900: (top row, left to right) The Royal Scots (Lothian Regiment), The Queen's (Royal West Surrey Regiment), The Buffs (East Kent Regiment); (centre row) The King's Own (Royal Lancaster Regiment), The Northumberland Fusiliers, The Royal Warwickshire Regiment; (bottom row) The Royal Fusiliers (City of London Regiment) (puggaree and field cap badges), The King's (Liverpool Regiment), The Norfolk Regiment.

Plate 15. Cap badges, 1900: (top row, left to right) The Royal Sussex Regiment, The Hampshire Regiment, The South Staffordshire Regiment; (centre row); The Dorsetshire Regiment, The Prince of Wales's Volunteers (South Lancashire Regiment), The Welsh Regiment; (bottom row) The Black Watch (Royal Highlanders), The Oxfordshire Light Infantry, The Essex Regiment.

Plate 16. Cap badges, 1900: (top row, left to right) The Duke of Edinburgh's (Wiltshire Regiment), The Manchester Regiment, The Prince of Wales's (North Staffordshire Regiment); (centre row) The York and Lancaster Regiment, The Durham Light Infantry, The Highland Light Infantry; (bottom row) The Seaforth Highlanders (Ross-shire Buffs, The Duke of Albany's), The Gordon Highlanders, The Queen's Own Cameron Highlanders.

Plate 17. Cap badges, 1900: (top row, left to right) The Royal Irish Rifles (field cap and puggaree badges), Princess Victoria's (Royal Irish Fusiliers), The Connaught Rangers; (centre row) Princess Louise's (Argyll and Sutherland Highlanders), The Prince of Wales's Leinster Regiment (Royal Canadians), The Royal Munster Fusiliers; (bottom row) The Royal Dublin Fusiliers, The Rifle Brigade (puggaree and field cap badges), The West India Regiment.

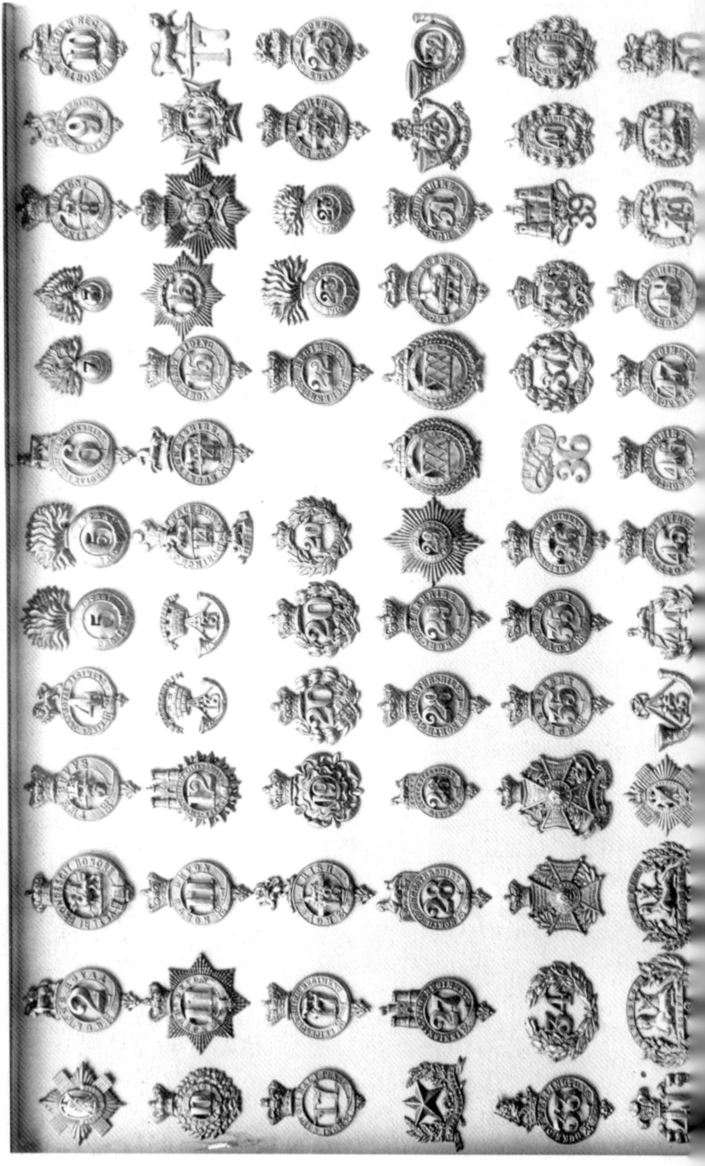

Plate 18. Other ranks' glengarry badges, 1874–81, 1st Foot to 50th Foot.

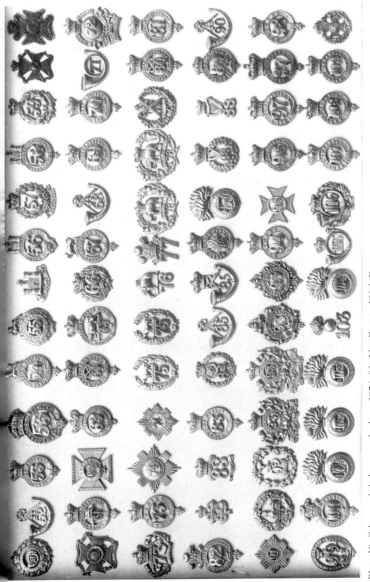

Plate 19. Other ranks' glengarry badges, 1874–81, 51st Foot to 109th Foot.

51

Plate 20. Cap badges of the British Army, 2000. *(Top row left to right)* The Life Guards, The Blues and Royals (Royal Horse Guards and 1st Dragoons), Royal Horse Artillery, 1st The Queen's Dragoon Guards, The Royal Scots Dragoon Guards (Carabiniers and Greys); *(second row)* The Queen's Royal Lancers, The Royal Tank Regiment, Royal Regiment of Artillery, Corps of Royal Engineers, Royal Corps of Signals; *(third row)* The Royal Scots (The Royal Regiment), The Royal Highland Fusiliers (Princess Margaret's Own Glasgow and Ayrshire Regiment), The King's Own Scottish Borderers, The Black Watch (Royal Highland Regiment), The Highlanders (Seaforth, Gordon and Cameron); *(fourth row)* The King's Regiment, The Prince of Wales's Own Regiment of Yorkshire, The Green Howards (Alexandra, Princess of Wales's Own Yorkshire Regiment), The Queen's Lancashire Regiment, The Duke of Wellington's Regiment (West Riding); *(fifth row)* The Royal Gloucestershire, Berkshire and Wiltshire Regiment, The Worcestershire and Sherwood Foresters Regiment, The Staffordshire Regiment (The Prince of Wales's), The Light Infantry, The Royal Green Jackets; *(sixth row)* Special Air Service Regiment, Army Air Corps, Royal Army Chaplain's Department (Christian), Royal Army Chaplain's Department (Jewish), Royal Logistic Corps.

Plate 21. Cap badges of the British Army, 2000. (Top row left to right) The Royal Dragoon Guards, The Queen's Royal Hussars (The Queen's Own and Royal Irish), 9th/12th Lancers (Prince of Wales's), The King's Royal Hussars, The Light Dragoons; (second row) Grenadier Guards, Coldstream Guards, Scots Guards, Irish Guards, Welsh Guards; (third row) The Argyll and Sutherland Highlanders (Princess Louise's), The Princess of Wales's Royal Regiment (Queen's and Royal Hampshires), The Royal Regiment of Fusiliers, The Royal Anglian Regiment, The King's Own Royal Border Regiment; (fourth row) The Royal Irish Regiment (27th Inniskilling, 83rd, 87th and Ulster Defence Regiment), The Devonshire and Dorset Regiment, The Cheshire Regiment, The Royal Welch Fusiliers, The Royal Regiment of Wales (24th/41st Foot); (fifth row) The Royal Gurkha Rifles, Queen's Gurkha Engineers, Queen's Gurkha Signals, The Queen's Own Gurkha Transport Regiment, The Parachute Regiment; (sixth row) Royal Army Medical Corps, Corps of Royal Electrical and Mechanical Engineers, The Adjutant General's Corps (SPS and ETS Branches), The Adjutant General's Corps (Provost Branch, MP) – Royal Military Police, The Adjutant General's Corps (Provost Branch, MPS) – Military Prison Service, The Adjutant General's Corps (ALS Branch) – Army Legal Service.

Plate 22a. Cap badges of the British Army, 2000. (Top row, left to right) Army Physical Training Corps, General Service Corps, Queen Alexandra's Royal Army Nursing Corps. (Bottom row, left to right) Royal Army Veterinary Corps, Small Arms School Corps, Royal Army Dental Corps, Intelligence Corps.

Plate 22b. Military pouches and ornaments. (Top) Rifle regiments. (Bottom) Life Guards.

Plate 23. Buttons. (Top row, left to right) Other ranks, 24th Foot, c.1805; officers, 24th Foot, c.1870; 56th Native Infantry, c.1830; 3rd Bengal Native Infantry, 1840–57. (Second row) Other ranks, 24th Foot, 1855–71; 57th Foot, 1855–71; 77th, 1855–71; The Middlesex Regiment, 1881–1959. (Third row) 2nd South Middlesex Rifle Volunteers, 1860–81; Royal East Middlesex Militia, 1855–81; The Earl of Chester's Yeomanry; Lord Lieutenants of Counties, the Commissioner of the Metropolitan Police and others. (Fourth row) Musicians; The South Wales Borderers, 1881–1955; anodised version, 1955–60; general service, 1871–1924. (Fifth row) Royal Artillery: 1795; 1833–8; 1838–56; Royal Horse Artillery, 1856–73.

Plate 24. Buttons of the 19th Foot, later The Green Howards. (Top row; left to right) Officers, up to 1795; small, pre-1795; officers, 1795–1825; officers, 1825–55. (Second row) Officers, 1855–61; officers, 1861–81; shell jacket button, 1855–70; officers, 1881–1903. (Third row) Other ranks, 1795–1855; other ranks, 1855–6; other ranks, 1856–72; small, 1856–72; small, 1951 to date. (Bottom row) Other ranks' general service button, 1872–1924; small, 1872–1924; cap, 1894–1924; other ranks, 1924–51; small, 1924–51; anodised other ranks' button, 1951 to date.

56

Fig. 34. Buttons (from left to right): 6th Dragoon Guards, up to 1881; 16th Lancers, 1830–61; other ranks, Militia General Service, 1871; officers, East York Militia, 1855–81.

the tunic was adopted in 1855, this design was retained with the Roman 'V' becoming '5' until 1922. The 2nd or Royal North British Dragoons (The Royal Scots Greys in 1877) adopted a button with a scalloped rim with the eagle on a tablet inscribed 'Waterloo' in the centre. Beneath this were the initials 'RNBD'. This button was retained on the tunic until 1877 when the letters were changed to 'RSG' because of the new title.

Another guide to the dating of buttons is the shank on the reverse. Until about 1840 this had been made by hand and then fitted, but by this date shanks were produced by machine in a uniform size and the backs of the buttons were invariably closed. At this period nearly every button was marked on the closed back with the maker's or tailor's name – another useful guide to dating.

In 1855, when the coatee and jackets of the cavalry were replaced with a tunic, the Hussars managed to retain an elementary form of frogging (cord ornamentation on the front of the jacket) but lost the five rows of buttons, which were replaced with a single row of plain domed brass buttons (gilt for officers). The 7th, 13th and 14th, the two last not dressed or titled as Hussars, retained their previous buttons until 1861, when they were converted to Hussars and adopted plain buttons. Except for the 2nd Dragoon Guards, 6th Dragoon Guards, 13th Light Dragoons, 14th Light Dragoons (mentioned above) and the 16th Lancers, the buttons adopted for wear on the tunic remained the same until at least 1900, when for the first time dress regulations (issued in that year) described the officers' buttons of each cavalry regiment. Until 1870 the 2nd Dragoon Guards had a button with the crown surmounting '2' over the initials of the regiment. In 1880 the button described in the list on page 58 was adopted. The 6th Dragoon Guards had a button with a leaf edge and the design shown in fig. 34. In 1881 they adopted the button described on page 58. The 7th had a button with a scalloped edge with a crown and the cypher 'VR' above 'QO' until 1861, while the 13th had a crown surmounting a rayed star with a circle in the centre with '13 LD'. Around the edge of the button were a number of battle honours. The 14th had a crown above '14 KLD' with a spray of laurels beneath and the honour 'Peninsula' above. The 16th Lancers retained the 1830 button (fig. 34) until 1861, when they adopted the pattern described on page 59.

Although dress regulations were issued throughout Queen Victoria's reign at various intervals, buttons were fully described only in those of 1900. Previously buttons were described as of regimental pattern with the proviso that 'The distinctions of regimental badges and devices and other peculiar distinctions which may have been granted under special authority to different regiments of cavalry are to be preserved'.

After the First World War a number of amalgamations took place in the cavalry and the blending of badges of both regiments naturally affected the button designs. The list on page 59, although taken from Dress Regulations of 1934, gives these details. Dates after the regimental titles are those of amalgamation.

Although Hussar regiments wore plain domed buttons on their full dress, some had 'badged' buttons. With the adoption of the 'frock' tunic for all but full-dress wear, the cavalry adopted for other ranks the GS or general service button (see plate 23). After 1924, when this pattern was abandoned by the entire army and a return made to regimental-pattern buttons, the Hussars adopted the designs of button detailed below.

Description of cavalry buttons (from Dress Regulations, 1900)

Household Cavalry
1st Life Guards. The letters 'LG' reversed and intertwined, surmounted by the crown with '1' beneath.
2nd Life Guards. The imperial crest between the letters 'LG' with '2' beneath. Edges scalloped.
Royal Horse Guards. The letters 'RHG' surmounted by a crown.
(Before 1860 the 2nd Life Guards had the crown over 'LG' with '2' beneath. In 1922 when the 1st and 2nd Life Guards amalgamated, the button of the 1st was adopted without a numeral.)

Dragoon Guards
1st. The star of the Order of the Garter surmounted by a crown. Inside, the letters 'KDG'.
2nd. As for 1st Dragoon Guards but with the word 'Bays'.
3rd. Garter with motto around the outer edge. Within, the Prince of Wales's plume. (For the field cap, the Garter is omitted and the plume is silver.)
4th. Star of the Order of St Patrick with 'RIDG' above the motto.
5th. As 1st but with the Garter inscribed '*Vestigia nulla retrorsum*' and inside '5', above 'DG'.
6th. Crowned Garter inscribed 'Carabineers'. Inside 'VI' over 'DG'.
7th. 'PRDG' surmounted by the Princess Royal's coronet.

Dragoons and Lancers
1st Dragoons. The royal crest inside a Garter inscribed 'Royal Dragoons'. (In 1904 the Garter contained '*Honi soit qui mal y pense*' and a scroll at the base of the button contained the title.)
2nd Dragoons. A scalloped-edged button with the eagle above 'Waterloo'. Below, the letters 'RSG'.
5th Lancers. On crossed lances, a circle surmounted by the crown with a

shamrock wreath below. On the circle 'Fifth Royal Lancers' and within it the harp.

6th Dragoons. Scalloped edge. Castle of Inniskilling with 'VI' below. For tunic and frock the design is in silver.

9th Lancers. On crossed lances surmounted by a crown, the letters 'AR' reversed and intertwined, with '9' beneath.

12th Lancers. Scalloped edge with the crown surmounting crossed lances with '12 ' resting on them.

16th Lancers. A crown over 'QL' with '16' beneath.

17th Lancers. Full dome button with death's head.

21st Lancers. Scalloped edge with a pair of upright lances with straps joined, intersecting 'XXI'. Above the middle number, the crown.

Hussars
All regiments are noted as having buttons full dome, gilt burnished.

Buttons of amalgamated cavalry regiments and Hussars (from Dress Regulations, 1934)

3rd/6th. 1920, upon crossed carbines the Prince of Wales's plume. Below the coronet, a scroll inscribed '3rd Carabiniers'.

4th/7th. 1922, 'IV-VII' surmounted by the Princess Royal's coronet.

5th Dragoon Guards/6th Dragoons. 1922, a circle inscribed with the motto of the 5th Dragoon Guards inside the Castle of Inniskilling with 'V' above, 'D' on the left and 'G' on the right.

16th/5th Lancers. 1922, the button of the 5th Lancers was adopted.

17th/21st Lancers. 1922, the button of the 17th was adopted but half ball.

3rd Hussars. Half ball, gilt burnished.

4th Hussars. Large buttons, ball, gilt burnished.

7th Hussars. Half ball, gilt burnished.

8th Hussars. Service dress and mess dress. Gilt burnished with 'KRIH' with 'VIII' beneath, surmounted by the crown. Undress buttons, full dome, gilt burnished.

10th Hussars. Large buttons – ball, gilt burnished with the Prince of Wales's plume over 'XRH'. Small buttons the same, but full dome.

11th Hussars. Service dress and mess dress. Flat gilt engraved with 'PAO' in monogram surmounted by a crown. Undress buttons full dome, gilt burnished.

13th/18th Hussars. 1920, full dome, gilt burnished.

14th/20th Hussars. 1920, flat gilt engraved with 'XIV' over 'XX' surmounted by a crown.

15th/19th Hussars. 1920, within the Garter and motto, the royal crest.

INFANTRY

After the order of 1767 that was fully detailed in the warrant of 1768, infantry regiments adopted the numbered button, with those of the officers following the lace, either silver or gold, while those of the other ranks were, until 1855, made of pewter. The earliest designs adopted seem to have been plain numbers, as intended by the order, but after only a few years differences were creeping in. At first these were confined to the decoration of the edge of the buttons, but soon they involved various designs on the face itself, usually in the form of a circle or circles around the centrally placed numeral.

The 1st Foot Guards (Grenadiers in 1815) had the crown above the

Fig. 35. Button, 3rd Foot Guards, 1790.

royal cypher, intertwined and reversed, while the Coldstream Guards had a star with a circle in the centre with 'Cm Gds'. The 3rd Foot Guards had 'Gds' with '3' beneath in a decorative edging but they changed, in about 1790, to the design shown in fig. 35 and a little later they changed again to one bearing the star of the Order of the Thistle, which had earlier been adopted by the officers. The Grenadier Guards in 1837 added the grenade to their buttons below the intertwined and reversed cypher beneath the crown. The Coldstream Guards had adopted the Garter star with the Garter inscribed 'Coldstream Guards' in about 1800 and still retain this pattern, but with '*Honi soit qui mal y pense*' in place of the name of the regiment (adopted about 1830). The Scots Guards still have the star of the Order of the Thistle on their buttons and the Grenadiers still retain the reversed and intertwined royal cypher with crown and small grenade.

According to the Royal Warrant of 1768, the following regiments of the line had gold lace and gilt buttons for officers: all regiments of Foot Guards; regiments of foot – 1, 7, 8, 11, 12, 18, 19, 21, 22, 23, 25, 27, 32, 36, 39, 40, 41, 42, 48, 49, 51, 53, 55, 57, 58, 59, 61, 62, 63, 64, 66, 69, 70. The rest of the infantry (numbered from 1 to 70 at this time) had silver lace and silver buttons for the officers. As well as the seventy line regiments noted in 1768, there were other units raised in times of war and disbanded when peace came. So short was the existence of some of these regiments that no details of their uniforms, badges or buttons are known.

By 1800 various established designs were in use, the most popular being the number in an open French scroll with a dot at the opening, or a crowned number in either a French scroll or circle or plain. Other buttons had the number on a circle or a wreath, some with plain edges, while others had roped or wreathed edges. Some designs incorporated battle honours or regimental distinctions while others, especially the Irish and Scottish, included the national emblem, the shamrock or thistle.

A great number of regiments, however, had their own peculiar designs, such as the 32nd Foot, which shortly after 1800 adopted a button that bore a crown surmounting a Garter composed of six circles with the number in the centre. Other ranks wore this button until 1871, officers until 1881. This pattern, but with four circles in the Garter, was briefly adopted about 1810 by the 43rd Foot.

The dating of infantry buttons is very difficult because the design worn by officers often differed from that of the men, and regiments changed and modified their designs during the later eighteenth and early nineteenth centuries. Dating a design is made more difficult at this time because makers' names do not narrow the span sufficiently to date within a decade. Fortunately many museums in Britain and abroad, notably in the United States and Gibraltar, have excavated examples of pewter and other buttons from barrack and camp sites. Once it has been ascertained when a certain regiment was quartered there, a reliable indication can be arrived at of the date of a particular design.

By 1830, when the lace colour of the entire army was changed to gold by William IV, most regiments had adopted the pattern of button they were to retain until the implementation of the Cardwell reforms and the recommendations of the 1877 Stanley Committee, which paired off most regiments in two-battalion regiments under territorial titles. Before the change to gold lace in 1830 these regiments had gold lace and gilt buttons: 1, 3, 4, 7, 8, 11, 12, 18, 19, 21, 22, 23, 25, 27, 32, 36, 39, 40, 41, 42, 48, 49, 51, 53, 55, 57, 58, 59, 64, 65, 69, 70, 73, 74, 78, 79, 80, 83, 86, 87, 89, 90, 91, 94, 98, 99. The rest of the infantry, numbered between 1 and 99, retained silver lace and buttons.

Rifle regiments had had white metal buttons but in 1833 black buttons were adopted by the 60th and the Rifle Brigade, silver and white metal buttons being used only by militia regiments. The 60th's buttons had the design of the number '60' within the strings of the bugle horn, above the bow a crown and below the bugle a spray of laurels. The Rifle Brigade's other ranks wore a button with the bugle horn surmounted by the crown, which covered the top of the strings, with the letters 'RB' within the strings.

Remembering that other ranks' buttons were pewter until the adoption of the tunic in 1855, the following list details the various designs worn before and after 1881. Many of the designs worn before 1855 were later used on the brass tunic buttons until 1871 for other ranks and 1881 for officers. Brass buttons, identical in design to the pewter ones, were manufactured before the introduction of the tunic with the idea of replacing the pewter ones, but the double-breasted tunic was issued before any great change could be made. It is not certain how many regiments were affected by this. Because of the change in regimental titles, it is easier to refer to each by number. The description of the post-1881 buttons is taken from Dress Regulations 1883, the first issued after the reforms of 1881. Details of regimental titles and numbers will be found on pages 19–24.

Other ranks of regular line regiments were issued in 1871 with a general service button that displayed the royal arms, regimental patterns being retained only by officers and senior NCOs until about 1924, when regimental buttons were again sanctioned for the rank and file.

The militia, who had silver buttons, retained their own designs based on their area or on traditional badges (fig. 34). In 1871 the rank and file of the militia were also ordered a general type of button with a scalloped edge with a crown in the centre (fig. 34). Both the officers' and the other ranks' buttons were in silver. In 1881, when the militia was incorporated as volunteer battalions of line regiments, they adopted the buttons of the parent regiment, but in silver. With the formation of the Territorial Force in 1908, all battalions wore the same buttons as the regular battalion, but in certain cases with slight differences such as the omission of battle honours.

Buttons of infantry regiments

1st. *c*.1840, star of the Order of the Thistle with around the bottom 'The Royal Regiment'. 1881, title 'The Royal Scots'.

2nd. Crowned star and Garter with 'Queen's Own' and '2' in the centre until *c*.1830, when replaced with plain white button with crown over '2'. 1881, within a circle surmounted by the crown, the Pascal lamb, within the circle 'The Royal West Surrey Regiment'. Beneath, a scroll inscribed 'The Queens'. At some period before 1900, the date 1661 was added beneath the lamb and in 1909 the design was replaced with the naval crown over the lamb and date 1661 with a scroll beneath 'The Queen's Royal Regt'.

3rd. 1830-81, a dragon on a roped bar with '3' beneath inside a circle inscribed *'Veteri frondescit honore'*. 1881, a crowned Garter, with the dragon within, inscribed 'The East Kent Regt, The Buffs', with the same motto as 1830–81 in a scroll beneath. In 1935 the circle was inscribed 'The Buffs, The Royal East Kent Regiment'.

4th. A crowned Garter with the lion of England inside. In the Garter 'King's Own Regiment'. Later 'IV' was added below the lion; this was changed to '4' in 1855. 1881, the lion of England with crown above and rose beneath in a circle inscribed 'The King's Own Royal Lancaster Regt'. In 1920 the word 'Lancaster' was omitted.

5th. 1836, George and the dragon within a Garter inscribed *'Quo fata vocant'*. Beneath central design, 'V', changed in 1855 to '5'. 1881, as before but without the '5'.

6th. Crowned Garter with motto *'Honi soit qui mal y pense'*. In the centre the antelope over '6'. *c*.1840, a collar and chain added to the antelope. 1881, Garter changed to a circle inscribed 'The Royal Warwickshire Regiment'.

7th. *c*.1810, crowned Garter with motto *'Honi soit qui mal y pense'*. Inside, the rose with '7' superimposed. 1881, as before but without the '7'.

8th. Crowned Garter with motto *'Honi soit qui mal y pense'*. Inside, the running horse over '8'. After 1855, for other ranks, a scroll inscribed 'King's' was placed beneath. 1881, a circle, surrounded by a laurel wreath, inscribed 'The Liverpool Regiment'. Within the circle, the running horse with scroll above *'Nec aspera terrent'*. A scroll on the base of the laurel wreath inscribed 'The King's'. In 1920 the circle was inscribed 'The King's Regiment' and a sphinx replaced the scroll on the laurel wreath.

9th. *c*.1830, number and crown within a circle with rays. After 1855, '9' with crown above in a single-line circle. 1881, Britannia holding an olive branch inside a circle (in some dies a Garter) inscribed 'The Norfolk Regiment' (or 'Regt'). 1935, Britannia alone appeared on the button.

10th. 1830, crowned over 'X' within an open laurel spray. In 1855 'X' changed to '10'. 1881, a crowned circle within an open laurel spray inscribed 'The Lincolnshire Regt'. Inside, the sphinx over 'Egypt'. 1946, 'Royal' added to the title.

11th. 1800, 'XI' within a crowned Garter inscribed 'Regiment' superimposed on a star. In 1855 'XI' changed to '11'. 1881, Garter inscribed 'The Devonshire Regt', and numeral replaced by the castle of Exeter.

12th. *c*.1810, crowned '12' within an open laurel spray. 1881, within a laurel wreath the castle and key with scroll above inscribed 'Gibraltar' and one beneath inscribed '*Montis insignia calpe*'. At the base of the laurel a scroll inscribed 'The Suffolk Regt'.

13th. 1842, a Garter, superimposed by a mural crown, inscribed 'Prince Albert's Lt. Infantry', the whole within an open laurel wreath. In the centre 'XIII', changed in 1855 to '13'. 1881, the numeral replaced by a stringed bugle horn and circle inscribed 'The Prince Albert's'.

14th. *c*.1838, the crown above the royal tiger with 'XIV' beneath. Above, a scroll inscribed 'India' and one beneath inscribed 'Waterloo'. In 1855 the honours appeared not in scrolls and the numeral was changed to '14'. 1881, the tiger within a circle inscribed 'India' and 'Waterloo'. Outside the circle, 'Prince of Wales's Own, West Yorkshire'.

15th. *c*.1820, '15' within a wreath in the centre of an eight-pointed star. 1881, the numeral replaced by the white rose.

16th. *c*.1810, crowned '16' within an open laurel wreath. 1881, on an eight-pointed star, a Maltese cross with superimposed a circle inscribed 'Bedfordshire'. Inside, a hart crossing a ford. 1919, a hart crossing a ford within a circle inscribed 'Bedfordshire and Hertfordshire'.

17th. 1830, crowned '17' within a continuous laurel wreath. 1881, within a laurel wreath, the royal tiger with scroll above inscribed 'Hindoostan' and one beneath 'Leicestershire'.

18th. 1800, crowned harp with '18' beneath. Around the edge, a wreath of shamrocks. 1881, within a shamrock wreath, a circle inscribed '*Virtutis namurcensis praemium*'. Within the circle, the crowned harp. 1922, disbanded.

19th. See plate 24.

20th. 1830, crowned 'XX' within a laurel wreath. In 1855 numeral changed to '20'. 1881, within a wreath of laurels, the sphinx over 'Egypt' with crown above.

21st. *c*.1830, thistle within a circle inscribed '*Nemo me impune lacessit*'. Other ranks had a different design. 1855, a crowned thistle with '21' on the ball. 1881, the thistle surmounted by the crown.

22nd. *c*.1810, '22' within a spray of oak leaves on an eight-pointed star. 1881, a circle inscribed 'The Cheshire Regiment' on an eight-pointed star within the circle and acorn and oak leaves.

23rd. *c*.1800, Prince of Wales's feathers with 'XXIII' beneath, all within a beaded edge. Officers' buttons *c*.1810, Prince of Wales's feathers within a crowned circle inscribed 'Royal Welch Fusiliers' with 'XXIII' beneath. 1855, buttons as other ranks *c*.1800 but with '23'. 1881, as 1855 but without numeral and around the edge inside the beading 'The Royal Welsh Fusiliers'. 1920, 'Welsh' changed to 'Welch'.

24th. *c*.1800, '24' within a continuous wreath. *c*.1810, as previous but button with scalloped edge. 1881, the Welsh dragon within a wreath of laurels.

25th. *c.*1820, a crown over '25' with around the edge of the button 'King's Own Borderers'. The word 'The' added *c.*1840. 1881, crown and numeral replaced by the royal crest. 1887, 'Scottish' added to the title.

26th. *c.*1830, '26' on a lined ground within a wreath. Edge scalloped. 1855, '26' within a continuous wreath. 1881 (linked in 1881 with 90th as rifle regiment), buttons, only on greatcoat, of a crowned bugle horn stringed within a thistle wreath. This pattern worn on service dress also.

27th. *c.*1775, a castle with three turrets flying St George's flag. Above 'Enniskilling' and beneath '27'. 1840, spelling changed to 'Inniskilling'. 1881 (linked with 108th), as previous but without numeral.

28th. *c.*1870, the king's crest above the cypher 'GR' (adopted *c.*1800 by other ranks). 'GR' replaced by '28' *c.*1830. 1881 (linked with 61st), within a laurel wreath inclined inwards, the royal crest above 'GR'.

29th. 1800, other ranks' button, '29' within a continuous circle. 1881 (linked with 36th) on an eight-pointed star a crowned circle inscribed 'The Worcestershire Regiment'. Below the circle a scroll inscribed 'Firm'. In the circle, the lion. 1909, star elongated and lion on a tablet inscribed 'Firm' within the Garter and motto '*Honi soit qui mal y pense*'.

30th. *c.*1840, a crowned Garter inscribed 'Cambridge' with a wreath of laurels around the edge. In the Garter 'XXX'. 1855, numeral changed to '30'. 1881 (linked with 59th), within a circle inscribed 'The East Lancashire Regiment' the sphinx over 'Egypt' above the rose of Lancaster.

31st. *c.*1840, a crowned Garter inscribed 'Huntingdonshire' with a wreath of roses, shamrocks and thistles around the edge. Inside the Garter 'XXXI', changed in 1555 to '31'. 1881 (linked with 70th), on an eight-pointed star, a crowned circle inscribed 'East Surrey' with two twigs of laurel on the lower bend. Within the circle, the arms of Guildford.

32nd. *c.*1820 (as described on page 61). 1881 (linked with 46th), within 'Duke of Cornwall's Light Infy' around the edge, a stringed bugle horn surmounted by the coronet. In 1929 the gateway of Launceston placed between the coronet and horn.

33rd. *c.*1800, other ranks' buttons had '33' within a roped rim. *c.*1840, '33' below a crown with a Garter round the edge inscribed 'Duke of Wellington's Regt'. 1881 (linked with 76th), around the edge, 'Duke of Wellington's West Riding Regt'. Inside, the elephant and howdah.

34th. *c.*1830, '34' within a wreath. 1881 (linked with 55th), within a laurel wreath, the dragon of China with scroll above inscribed 'China'. Around the edge 'The Border Regiment'.

35th. 1832, '35' within a crowned Garter inscribed 'Royal Sussex Regt'. 1881 (linked with 107th), a crowned Garter inscribed 'Royal Sussex Regt', within a lined cross, the whole superimposed on a star. Scalloped edge. 1884, Maltese cross within a circle inscribed 'Royal Sussex Regt'. In the centre of the cross a wreath with the cross of St George.

36th. *c.*1830, crowned '36' within an open French scroll with dot at opening. 1881, linked with 29th.

37th. *c.*1830, crowned '37' within a laurel wreath. 1881 (linked with 67th), within a laurel wreath the royal tiger; below the tiger the Hampshire rose.

38th. *c.*1800, crowned '38' above the Staffordshire knot. 1881 (linked with 80th), the Staffordshire knot with crown above.

39th. *c.*1800, crowned '39' with a French circle with dot. 1881 (linked with

54th), the castle and key with above 'Gibraltar' and beneath '*Primus in Indis*'. Around the top edge 'The Dorsetshire Regt'. Beneath the bottom scroll, the sphinx on a tablet inscribed 'Marabout'.

40th. *c*.1800, '40' within an open spray of leaves. 1881 (linked with 82nd), within a laurel wreath with scroll at the base inscribed 'The Prince of Wales's Vols', a crowned circle inscribed 'The South Lancashire Regiment'. Inside, the Prince of Wales's feathers over the sphinx and 'Egypt'.

41st. *c*.1831, buttons bore the Prince of Wales's feathers and coronet with '41' and motto '*Gwell augau neu chivillydd*'. 1855, the Prince of Wales's feathers and coronet above '41'. 1881 (linked with 69th), on a circle surmounted by a crown, within a laurel wreath, 'The Welsh Regiment' inside the Prince of Wales's feathers. 1920, 'Welsh' changed to 'Welch'.

42nd. *c*.1810, the star of the Order of the Thistle with '42' in the centre. 1881 (linked with 73rd), the star of the Order of the Thistle with St Andrew and cross in the centre. Around the edge of button, 'The Royal Highlanders The Black Watch'. 1934, title around the edge omitted. 1855–71, other ranks had plain '42' on buttons.

43rd. *c*.1810, '43' within a laurel wreath. Officers' buttons *c*.1810, see page 61. *c*.1830, the officers' buttons had a crowned bugle horn with '43' between the strings. Although the other ranks' button was adopted after 1855, this design continued to be worn unofficially. 1881 (linked with 52nd), scalloped edge. Within a laurel wreath, a bugle horn stringed above the word 'Oxfordshire'. *c*.1908, title changed to 'Oxfordshire and Buckinghamshire'.

44th. *c*.1825, '44' beneath a crown. 1881 (linked with 56th), within an oak-leaf wreath, the badge of the county of Essex with the sphinx over 'Egypt' above and the castle and key below. 1902, the badge of the county of Essex replaced by an eagle on a roped bar.

45th. *c*.1820, crowned '45' within a French scroll with dot. 1881 (linked with 95th), a crowned Maltese cross with a wreath in the centre. In the wreath a stag lodged. On the left division 'Sherwood', on the right 'Foresters' and on the bottom 'Derbyshire'. 1902, title changed to 'Notts & Derby'.

46th. 1855, '46' within a French scroll with dot. 1881, linked with 32nd.

47th. *c*.1819, crown with lion above in an open wreath of leaves. In the opening 'Tarifa'. 1881 (linked with 81st), within a circle inscribed 'Loyal North Lancashire', the arms of the city of Lancaster surmounted by the royal crest. 1902, circle replaced by wreath and title placed outside with 'Tarifa' above the royal crest.

48th. *c*.1810, crowned '48' on a twisted bar (for other ranks). 1881 (linked with 58th), within a scroll inscribed 'The Northamptonshire Regiment', the castle and key with crown above.

49th. *c*.1818, within a Union wreath, the crowned Garter inscribed 'P. Charlotte of Wales'. Within '49'. 1881 (linked with 66th), a crowned circle inscribed 'P. Charlotte of Wales', within the dragon of China above 'R. Berks'. 1959, officers' buttons displayed the dragon only mounted in silver.

50th. 1831, the royal crest with '50' beneath (other ranks). 1885, for all. 1881 (linked with 97th), the royal crest.

51st. 1855, within a scalloped button a wreath with '51'. 1881 (linked with 105th), scalloped edge. Within a wreath a French horn with rose in the centre and crown above. 1895, scalloped edge and wreath omitted.

52nd. 1855, scalloped edge. '52' within an open wreath. 1881, linked with 43rd.

53rd. 1855, '53' within a Garter inscribed 'Shropshire' in an eight-pointed star. 1881 (linked with 85th), a crowned circle inscribed 'Shropshire' with twigs of laurel at the base. Within the monogram 'KLI'.

54th. *c*.1805, crowned '54' within an open laurel wreath. 1881, linked with 39th.

55th. *c*.1840, crowned Chinese dragon above '55' within an open laurel wreath. 1881, linked with 34th.

56th. *c*.1800, crowned '56' within a laurel wreath. 1881, linked with 44th.

57th. 1830, '57' beneath the honour 'Albuera' within a laurel wreath. 1881, (linked with 77th), within a wreath of laurels, the Prince of Wales's plume. On the base of the wreath a scroll inscribed 'Albuera'.

58th. *c*.1800, '58' within a circle inscribed 'Gibraltar, Egypt, Maida'. 1881, linked with 48th.

59th. 1840, crowned '59' within a single circle (other ranks). 1855, for all. 1881, linked with 30th.

60th. See page 61. 1881, within a laurel wreath a bugle with strings with the crown above.

61st. Crowned '61' within a single line circle. 1881, linked with 28th.

62nd. 1800, '62' within a French circle with dot. 1881 (linked with 99th), the cypher of HRH The Duke of Edinburgh with coronet above and 'Wiltshire Regiment' below.

63rd. *c*.1780, '63' in the centre of an eight-pointed star. 1881 (linked with 96th), crowned Garter with motto. Within, the sphinx over 'Egypt'.

64th. 1830, crowned '64' (other ranks). 1855, for all. 1881 (linked with 98th), within a laurel wreath with scroll inscribed 'Prince of Wales's' a crowned circle inscribed 'The North Staffordshire Regiment'. Within, the Staffordshire knot.

65th. '65' within a raised single line (other ranks). 1881 (linked with 84th), a scroll inscribed 'York and Lancaster Regiment'. At the opening a coronet. Inside, the royal tiger within an open laurel wreath with a rose at the base.

66th. 1830, '66' beneath a crown, in a laurel wreath. 1855, crowned '66' in a single line circle. 1881, linked with 49th.

67th. 1810, '67' within a French scroll with dot (other ranks). 1855, for all. 1881, linked with 37th.

68th. 1830, crowned bugle horn with '68' between the strings. 1881 (linked with 106th), bugle with crown above.

69th. 1830, crowned '69' within a laurel wreath. 1881, linked with 41st.

70th. *c*.1850, '70' within a single line circle. 1881, linked with 31st.

71st. *c*.1825, crowned French horn with '71' in the curl. 1881 (linked with 74th), star of the Order of the Thistle with in the centre the French horn with monogram 'HLI' in the curl. Beneath the horn a scroll with 'Assaye' and above it the crown as in the order of the Star of India. Beneath the scroll, an elephant.

72nd. *c*.1800, crowned '72' within a single line circle. 1881 (linked with 78th), a stag's head with the cypher of HRH The Duke of Connaught above, with scroll beneath inscribed 'Seaforth Highlanders'.

73rd. 1820, crowned '73' within an open spray of roses and thistles. 1840, '73' within a crowned circle with honours 'Seringapatam' and 'Mangalore'. At the base a scroll inscribed 'Waterloo'. 1855, pre-1840 pattern reverted to. 1881, linked with 42nd.

74th. 1830, crown above the elephant over '74' within an open laurel wreath. At the opening the word 'Assaye'. 1881, linked with 71st.

75th. *c*.1811, crowned '75', within an open spray of thistles. 1881 (linked with 92nd), the cross of St Andrew, a circle inscribed 'Gordon Highlanders' on the upper half and covered on the lower half by thistle wreath. On the cross at the top, the sphinx over 'Egypt' above the royal tiger over 'India'.

76th. 1830, elephant over '76', with around the honours 'Hindoostan' and 'Peninsula'. 1855, howdah appears on elephant's back. 1881, linked with 33rd.

77th. *c*.1830 (see plate 23). 1881, linked with 57th.

78th. *c*.1840, crown over the elephant above '78'. A laurel wreath at the base and the honours 'Assaye', 'Maida' and 'Java' at the top. 1881, linked with 72nd.

79th. 1800, crowned Garter with motto '*Nemo me impune lacessit*' with '79' within. Beneath, a spray of thistles and each side one letter of the royal cypher (depending on reign). 1881, crowned thistle with 'The Queen's Own Cameron Highlanders' around the outer edge.

80th. *c*.1820, crowned Staffordshire knot above '80' within an open laurel wreath. 1881, linked with 38th.

81st. *c*.1812, '81' within a circle inscribed 'Maida' at the top and 'Corunna' at the base. Between the honours, a small rose. 1881, linked with 47th.

82nd. *c*.1820, '82' below the Prince of Wales's plume. 1881, linked with 40th.

83rd. *c*.1830, crowned '83' within a laurel wreath. 1881 (linked with 86th), black button, with scalloped edge. A crowned harp above a scroll, with shamrock leaves each end, inscribed 'Royal Irish Rifles'.

84th. 1809, '84' below a ducal coronet with rose beneath inside an open wreath of laurels. 1881, linked with 65th.

85th. 1821, a crowned circle, on an eight-pointed star, inscribed 'King's Light Infantry', within the circle '85'. 1881, linked with 53rd.

86th. 1832, scalloped edge. Crowned Irish harp above '86' (officers'). Other ranks had the crowned Garter inscribed 'Royal County Down' with harp inside. 1855, officers' pattern adopted by all. 1881, linked with 83rd.

87th. 1855, scalloped edge with eagle on a tablet above '87'. This design was worn before 1855 by other ranks. 1881, linked with 89th.

88th. *c*.1800, '88' within a French scroll with dot. 1860, design changed for officers to button with scalloped edge with numeral within a crowned circle inscribed 'Connaught Rangers' with a wreath of shamrocks. At the base, the motto '*Quis separabit*' and a harp. 1881 (linked with 94th), scalloped edge with an elephant below a harp within a wreath of shamrocks. 1894, design changed to a wreath of shamrocks and the crowned harp. At the base a scroll inscribed '*Quis separabit*'. 1922, disbanded.

89th. *c*.1810, '89' within a French scroll with dot. (Also a version without dot.) 1866, officers' buttons changed to a pattern with the coronet of Queen Victoria above the number at the opening of the scroll. 1881 (linked with 87th), scalloped edge. An eagle with a wreath of laurels (referred to as the Barrosa eagle as it was a French colour captured in the battle). Below the eagle, a tablet inscribed '8'.

90th. *c*.1800, '90' in a single line circle. 1881, linked with 26th.

91st. *c*.1830, crowned '91' within a single line circle. Inside the edge of the circle, 'Argyllshire Regiment' (officers). 1855, for all. 1863, officers' pattern changed to a crowned circle inscribed 'Argyllshire Regiment' with '91' at the bottom. Within the circle, St Andrew and cross. 1881 (linked with 93rd), within a myrtle wreath interlaced with a wreath of butcher's broom, a boar's head in a scroll inscribed '*Ne obliviscaris*' in the wreath of butcher's broom, a cat on a scroll inscribed '*Sans peur*'. A label of three points above the boar's head and the cat, and the coronet of Princess Louise above the wreaths.

92nd. c.1800, '92' within a single line circle. c.1835, the numeral surmounted by a crown. 1855, crown omitted. 1881, linked with 75th.

93rd. c.1814, crowned '93'. 1881, linked with 91st.

94th. 1832, crowned '94' within a single line circle. 1881, linked with 88th.

95th. 1855, '95' and crown within a single line circle. 1881, linked with 45th.

96th. 1824, crowned '96' within a French scroll. In 1830, officers' pattern changed to a crowned Garter with motto with '96' inside. 1881, linked with 63rd.

97th. 1855, crowned '97' within a French scroll. 1881, linked with 50th.

98th. c.1830, scalloped rim. Crowned '98'. Officers' version had an almost Tudor crown. 1881, linked with 64th.

99th. c.1830, '99' beneath an ornamental crown with cut rim. 1855, crowned '99', within a French scroll. 1874, officers' button crowned '99' above a scroll inscribed 'Duke of Edinburgh's Regt'. 1881, linked with 62nd.

100th. 1858 raised, Prince of Wales's feathers, coronet and motto above '100', all within a Garter inscribed 'Prince of Wales's Royal Canadian Regt'. 1881, linked with 109th, a circle inscribed 'Prince of Wales's Leinster Regiment' with, inside, the Prince of Wales's plume, coronet and motto. 1922, disbanded.

NOTE: the 101st to 109th were transferred from the Honourable East India Company armies to the British Army in 1861.

101st. A grenade with '101' on the ball. Around lower edge of button 'Royal Bengal Fusiliers'. 1881 (linked with 104th), within 'Royal Munster Fusiliers' around the edge, the tiger on the ball of the grenade. 1922, disbanded.

102nd. Crown over the royal tiger with '102' below. Around the edge 'Royal Madras Fusiliers'. 1881 (linked with 103rd), within 'Royal Dublin Fusiliers' the grenade with crown on the ball. 1922, disbanded.

103rd. As 101st but with change in number and 'Bombay' for 'Bengal'. 1881, linked with 102nd.

104th. As 101st but with change in number and omission of 'Royal'. 1881, linked with 101st.

105th. Crowned French horn with 'CV' in the curl, changed to '105' before 1881. 1881, linked with 51st.

106th. Crowned French horn with '106' in the curl. Beneath, 'Bombay Light Infantry'. 1881, linked with 68th.

107th. '107' in a plain Garter within a laurel wreath on a Maltese cross with top edge inscribed 'Bengal' and bottom edge 'Infantry'. 1881, linked with 35th.

108th. Crowned Garter inscribed 'Madras Infantry' with '108' inside. 1881, linked with 27th.

109th. Crowned '109' above 'Bombay Infantry'. 1881, linked with 100th.

ARTILLERY AND SUPPORTING TROOPS
Artillery

The first pattern of button, dating from about 1767, had the design of a cannon on its carriage facing right with a pile of shot in front, the whole within a roped rim. As was usual at this date, the metal face was fitted to a wooden or bone back. In about 1785 a button displaying the shield of the Board of Ordnance was adopted for wear (see plate 23, fifth row, left). The officers' buttons were gilt, while those of the other ranks were bronze.

About 1802 a new pattern was worn. This consisted of a crowned Garter inscribed 'Royal Regt of Artillery' with, inside, the reversed and intertwined cypher. About 1808 The Royal Horse Artillery, which had been formed in 1793 and had worn the same design as the Royal Artillery but on a ball button, adopted a design of a crowned Garter inscribed 'Royal Horse Artillery' or 'Royal Horse Artil' or Royal Horse Arty'. Inside was the royal cypher. This pattern continued to be worn until 1855 on the jacket, although it was retained until 1912 on the greatcoat.

In 1833 the Royal Artillery adopted a button with the crown surmounting three guns (see plate 23), which in 1838 had the addition of a scroll beneath with '*Ubique*' and a scalloped edge (plate 23). This pattern was abandoned in 1855 and both Royal Artillery and Royal Horse Artillery bore the crown over three guns on their buttons until 1873, when both adopted the device of the crown over a single field gun.

Volunteer and militia artillery wear a variety of white metal buttons that incorporate the badge worn by the regular regiment but with the addition of titles.

Corps and others

Most of the corps had a variety of titles during their history. They were sometimes considered military but at other times were described in dress regulations under 'Civilian Departments'.

The Royal Corps of Transport, for example, originated as the Corps of Royal Waggoners in 1794. It was disbanded the following year, but re-raised as the Royal Waggon Corps in 1799. In 1802 the title was changed to 'Royal Waggon Train' (fig. 36), and it was disbanded in 1833. When it was once more resurrected just before the Crimean War of 1854, it was as the Land Transport Corps, changed again in 1857 to 'Military Train', a title that lasted until 1869, when it was altered to 'Army Service Corps'. This, however, was only a corps of other ranks, officers being supplied from 1859 to 1864 by the Commissariat Staff Corps, from 1864 to 1875 by the Control Department, from 1875 to 1880 by the Commissariat and Transport Department, from 1880 to 1881 by the Commissariat and Transport Staff (fig. 36), and from 1881 until it was merged with the other ranks to form one corps (fig. 36) by the Commissariat and Transport Corps. In 1918, as a result of its war work, it was granted the prefix 'Royal'. The RASC became The Royal Corps of Transport in 1965.

The Royal Engineers have a similar pedigree, consisting of two bodies, one of officers and the other of men (Royal Sappers and Miners), merged in 1856 to form the Corps of Royal Engineers.

The Royal Army Medical Corps also consisted of two separate bodies until 1898, when the Army Medical Department merged with the Medical Staff Corps to form the Royal Army Medical Corps.

Fig. 36. Buttons: (left) Commissariat and Transport Staff, 1880–1; (centre) Royal Waggon Train, 1802; (right) Army Service Corps, 1881–1918.

The Royal Army Ordnance Corps is perhaps the most complicated of all, dating back to the formation of the Board of Ordnance in 1418. In 1877, however, the Ordnance Stores Branch was formed. In 1881 this became the Ordnance Stores Corps and in 1896 amalgamated with the Stores Companies of the Service Corps to form the Army Ordnance Corps. It was granted the prefix 'Royal' in 1918.

Most of the corps or department buttons of the nineteenth century will be found bearing the title, usually in a Garter with the royal crest or either the star of the Order of the Garter or the royal cypher inside. Careful research into the dates of changes in title of the corps or department will enable the collector to date buttons with far more certainty than those of the cavalry or infantry.

There are numerous other types of button worn by personnel attached to the royal household and by non-regimental officers and general officers.

Cap badges. Fig. 37. (Left) Wessex Brigade, 1958. Fig. 38. (Right) Highland Brigade, 1958.

4. Badges and buttons from 1958 to the present

In 1958 the British Army was streamlined – the first reorganisation since the Second World War. As had been done after the First World War with the cavalry, there were amalgamations of regiments; some regiments had the number of their battalions reduced and others were disbanded, as with the Irish infantry regiments in 1922. This was the start of the process of modernising and shrinking the Army to suit changing needs, a process that continued until the end of the twentieth century.

The cavalry in 1958

Most of the cavalry regiments that had escaped amalgamation in 1922 were affected by amalgamation in 1958. Regiments affected were:

Dragoon Guards
1st and 2nd to form 1st The Queen's Dragoon Guards (1959). Badge, plate 20 and fig. 44 (1st DG); collar badge, plate 3b (2nd DG) but smaller. Buttons as described on page 58 but 'QDG' in place of 'KDG'.

Hussars
3rd and 7th to form The Queen's Own Hussars (1958). Badge, plate 4 (3rd Hussars) but with scroll reading 'The Queen's Own Hussars'; collar badge, crowned and reversed and intertwined cypher 'QO' with title on scroll beneath.
4th and 8th to form The Queen's Royal Irish Hussars (1958). Badge, crowned harp on a circle inscribed with the title and with a scroll beneath the circle inscribed '*Mente et manu*'; collar badge the same but smaller, in pairs with harp facing inwards. Badge, fig. 42. Buttons, plain gilt domed.

Lancers
9th and 12th to form the 9th/12th Royal Lancers (Prince of Wales's) (1960). Badge, crowned Prince of Wales's feathers on crossed lances with scroll over the butts inscribed 'IX–XII'; collar badge, the same but smaller. Fig. 48. Buttons, reversed and intertwined cypher 'AR' with crown above on crossed lances.

The infantry in 1958

The changes to the infantry were more traumatic. It was grouped into brigades, a system that was never liked but lasted for twelve years. The main objection was the loss of the regiment's cherished cap badges and the substitution of brigade cap badges in 'Staybright', an anodised aluminium metal.

Lowland Brigade. The Royal Scots, The Royal Highland Fusiliers [1959,

Cap badges. Fig. 39. (Left) Royal Armoured Corps, 1941. Fig. 40. (Right) The Devonshire and Dorset Regiment, 1971.

from The Royal Scots Fusiliers and The Highland Light Infantry], The King's Own Scottish Borderers, and The Cameronians. Badge: circle inscribed '*Nemo me impune lacessit*', with thistle inside, the whole on the cross of St Andrew.

Home Counties Brigade. The Queen's Royal Surrey Regiment [1959, from The Queen's Royal Regiment (West Surrey) and The East Surrey Regiment], The Queen's Own Buffs, The Royal Kent Regiment [1961, from The Buffs (Royal East Kent Regiment) and The Queen's Own Royal West Kent Regiment], The Royal Sussex Regiment, The Middlesex Regiment. Badge: sword pointing upwards behind a Saxon crown with scroll inscribed 'Home Counties'.

Lancastrian Brigade. The King's Own Royal Border Regiment [1959, from The King's Own Royal Regiment (Lancaster) and The Border Regiment], The King's Regiment (Manchester and Liverpool) [1958, from The King's Regiment (Liverpool) and The Manchester Regiment], The Lancashire Regiment [1958, from The East Lancashire Regiment, The South Lancashire Regiment (The Prince of Wales's Volunteers) and The Loyal Regiment]. Badge: royal crest on a rose within a laurel wreath with scroll beneath inscribed 'Lancastrian'.

Fusilier Brigade. The Royal Northumberland Fusiliers, The Royal Fusiliers, and The Lancashire Fusiliers. Badge: brass grenade with George and the Dragon within a laurel wreath.

Midland Brigade (later changed to **Forester Brigade**). The Royal Warwickshire Regiment, The Royal Leicestershire Regiment, The Sherwood Foresters. Badge: within the Garter a hart crossing a ford; beneath, a scroll inscribed 'Forester Brigade'.

East Anglian Brigade. 1st East Anglian Regiment [1959, from The Royal Norfolk Regiment and The Suffolk Regiment], 2nd East Anglian Regiment [1960, from The Royal Lincolnshire Regiment and The Northamptonshire Regiment], 3rd East Anglian Regiment [1958, from The Bedfordshire and Hertfordshire Regiment and The Essex Regiment]. Badge: on an eight-pointed star the castle and key of Gibraltar with scroll beneath inscribed 'East Anglian'.

Wessex Brigade. The Devonshire and Dorset Regiment [1958, from The Devonshire Regiment and The Dorset Regiment], The Gloucestershire

*Cap badges.
Fig. 41. The
Royal Hussars
(Prince of
Wales's Own),
1969–1992.
Fig. 42.(Right)
The Queen's
Royal Irish
Hussars,
1958–1993.*

Regiment, The Royal Hampshire Regiment, The Duke of Edinburgh's Royal Regiment [1959, from The Royal Berkshire Regiment (Princess Charlotte of Wales's) and The Wiltshire Regiment (Duke of Edinburgh's)]. Badge: see fig. 37.

Light Infantry Brigade. The Somerset and Cornwall Light Infantry [1959, from The Somerset Light Infantry (Prince Albert's) and The Duke of Cornwall's Light Infantry], The King's Own Yorkshire Light Infantry, The King's Shropshire Light Infantry, The Durham Light Infantry. Badge: stringed bugle horn.

Yorkshire Brigade. The Prince of Wales's Own Regiment of Yorkshire [1958, from The West Yorkshire Regiment (The Prince of Wales's Own) and The East Yorkshire Regiment (The Duke of York's)], The Green Howards, The Duke of Wellington's Regiment, The York and Lancaster Regiment. Badge: crowned rose with scroll beneath inscribed 'Yorkshire'.

Mercian Brigade. The Cheshire Regiment, The Worcestershire Regiment, The Staffordshire Regiment [1959, from The South Staffordshire Regiment and The North Staffordshire Regiment (Prince of Wales's)]. Badge: double-headed eagle surmounted by a Saxon crown.

Welsh Brigade. The Royal Welsh Fusiliers, The South Wales Borderers, The Welch Regiment. Badge: the Prince of Wales's feathers, coronet and motto.

North Irish Brigade. The Royal Inniskilling Fusiliers, The Royal Ulster Rifles, The Royal Irish Rifles. Badge: crowned angel harp with scroll beneath inscribed 'North Irish Brigade'.

Highland Brigade. The Black Watch, The Queen's Own Highlanders (Seaforth and Cameron) [1961, from The Seaforth Highlanders (Ross-shire Buffs, The Duke of Albany's) and The Queen's Own Cameron Highlanders], The Gordon Highlanders, The Argyll and Sutherland Highlanders. Badge: see fig. 38.

Green Jackets Brigade. 1st Green Jackets [1958, from The Oxfordshire and Buckinghamshire Light Infantry], 2nd Green Jackets [1958, from The King's Royal Rifle Corps] and 3rd Green Jackets [1958, from The Rifle Brigade (Prince Consort's Own)]. Badge: Maltese cross with tablet above inscribed 'Peninsula' with superimposed bugle horn stringed; the whole surrounded by a crowned laurel wreath.

The cavalry 1969–71

Starting in 1969, yet more amalgamations were made to cavalry regiments. Those affected were regiments that had escaped

Cap badges. Fig. 43. (Left) The Household Cavalry Regiment, 1993. (The Life Guards; The Blues and Royals.) Fig. 44. (Right) 1st The Queen's Dragoon Guards, 1993.

amalgamation in 1922 and 1958. For the first time since the 1st and 2nd Life Guards were amalgamated in 1922, the other regiment of The Household Cavalry, The Royal Horse Guards, was affected.

In 1969 The Royal Horse Guards and the 1st Dragoons were amalgamated to form **The Blues and Royals**. The badge was as for The Royal Horse Guards but with 'Blues and Royals' in a circle (fig. 43, right). The buttons have a crown over 'RHO' above '1st D'.

In the same year the 10th Hussars and the 11th Hussars were amalgamated to form **The Royal Hussars (Prince of Wales's Own)**. For the badge see fig. 41. The buttons were flat gilt with the Prince of Wales's feathers.

In 1971 the 3rd/6th Dragoon Guards and the 2nd Dragoons were amalgamated to form **The Royal Scots Dragoon Guards (Carabiniers and Greys)**. The badge featured the eagle of the 2nd Dragoons with crossed carbines and title scroll (plate 20, top row, and fig. 45).

The infantry 1966–70

By 1970 the brigade system had broken up and some large regiments had been formed, each with its own cap and collar badges. Regiments amalgamated to implement the brigade system had new badges while those unaffected resumed their old ones. In January 1970 The Royal Scots, The Black Watch, The Argyll and Sutherland Highlanders, The King's Own Scottish Borderers, The Duke of Wellington's Regiment, The Green Howards, The Cheshire Regiment and The Royal Welsh Fusiliers resumed their old cap badges. One of the first brigades to disappear was the Home Counties Brigade; in 1966 the four regiments within it became the 1st to 4th Battalions, The Queen's Regiment. In 1964 the Anglian Brigade disappeared to be replaced by four battalions of The Royal Anglian Regiment. In 1966 the Green Jackets Brigade became The Royal Green Jackets and in 1971 the Lancastrian Brigade split into three regiments: The Queen's Lancashire Regiment [The Lancashire Regiment (Prince of

Cap badges. Fig. 45. (Left) The Royal Scots Dragoon Guards (Carabiniers and Greys), 1993. Fig. 46. (Right) The Royal Dragoon Guards, 1993.

Wales's Volunteers) and The Loyal Regiment (North Lancashire)], The King's Regiment and The Royal Border Regiment. The Fusilier Brigade was converted to The Royal Regiment of Fusiliers with three battalions.

By 1971 the split was complete and by means of various amalgamations, such as that of The South Wales Borderers and The Welch Regiment in 1969 to form The Royal Regiment of Wales (the new regiment retained the old Welsh Brigade badge), the infantry of the line, which in 1881 had sixty-nine regiments, was reduced to twenty-nine by amalgamations and disbanding (The Cameronians and The York and Lancaster Regiment were disbanded in 1968).

From 1968 all infantry regiments were grouped into divisions, such as The Guards Division, The Scottish Division, The Queen's Division and so on, but this has no effect on cap badges.

The various badges described above are all made in 'Staybright' or anodised aluminium, which, unlike the earlier brass or white metal badges, needs no cleaning and has the appearance of glittery tinfoil. This new metal, also used for buttons, was introduced in 1952 and is now universally issued.

The British Army 1990-4

There were some years of stability until the early 1990s, when the 'Options for Change' scheme was implemented to reduce manpower and streamline the Army. This radically affected the regiments as reductions and amalgamations were made, resulting in a smaller and more efficient force. The new regiments and their badges, if new, are listed below.

Although the restructuring of the Army started with 'Options for Change' in 1990, because of significant changes in the strategic setting the scope of the reorganisation has been extended. This involves a reduction of about one-quarter of the total of 119,000 men, which affects the number and sizes of regiments. Regiments or battalions have, therefore, been amalgamated or put into suspended animation.

The Army for 1994 was composed of the following regiments. The list includes the regiments they were formed from and the date of amalgamation.

Cap badges. Fig. 47. (Left) The Queen's Royal Hussars (The Queen's Own and Royal Irish), 1993. Fig. 48. (Right) 9th/12th Royal Lancers (Prince of Wales's), 1993.

CAVALRY

The Household Cavalry and the Royal Armoured Corps

The Household Cavalry Regiment. Formed 1992 from **The Life Guards** (fig. 43, left) and **The Blues and Royals** (fig. 43, right).

1st The Queen's Dragoon Guards. Fig. 44.

The Royal Scots Dragoon Guards. Fig. 45.

The Royal Dragoon Guards. Fig. 46. Formed 1992 from 4th/7th The Royal Dragoon Guards and 5th Royal Inniskilling Dragoon Guards.

The Queen's Royal Hussars (The Queen's Own and Royal Irish). Fig. 47. Formed 1993 from The Queen's Own Hussars and The Queen's Royal Irish Hussars.

9th/12th Lancers (Prince of Wales's). Fig. 48.

The King's Royal Hussars. Fig. 50. Formed 1992 from The Royal Hussars and 14th/20th King's Hussars.

The Light Dragoons. Fig. 49. Formed 1992 from 13th/18th Royal Hussars and 15th/19th The King's Royal Hussars.

The Queen's Royal Lancers. Fig. 51. Formed 1993 from 16th/5th The Queen's Royal Lancers and 17th/21st Lancers.

1st Royal Tank Regiment. Fig. 52. Formed 1993 from 1st and 4th Royal Tank Regiments.

2nd Royal Tank Regiment. Fig. 52. Formed 1992 from 2nd and 3rd Royal Tank Regiments.

FOOT GUARDS

1st Battalion Grenadier Guards (2nd Battalion in suspended animation 1994). Plate 21.

1st Battalion Coldstream Guards (2nd Battalion in suspended animation 1993). Plate 21.

Cap badges. Fig. 49. (Left) The Light Dragoons, 1993. Fig. 50. (Right) The King's Royal Hussars, 1993.

Cap badges.
Fig. 51. (Left)
The Queen's
Royal Lancers,
1993.
Fig. 52. (Right)
1st and 2nd
Regiments The
Royal Tank
Regiment, 1993.

1st Battalion Scots Guards (2nd Battalion in suspended animation 1993). Plate 21.
1st Battalion Irish Guards. Plate 21.
1st Battalion Welsh Guards. Plate 21.

INFANTRY
1st Battalion The Royal Scots. Plates 14, top row, and 20.
1st Battalion The Royal Highland Fusiliers. Plate 20.
1st Battalion The King's Own Scottish Borderers. Plates 7 and 20.
1st Battalion The Black Watch. Plates 15, bottom row, and 20.
1st Battalion The Highlanders (Seaforth, Gordon and Cameron). Formed in 1994 from The Queen's Own Highlanders and The Gordon Highlanders. Plate 20.
1st Battalion The Argyll and Sutherland Highlanders. Plates 17, centre row, and 21.
1st/2nd Battalion The Princess of Wales's Royal Regiment. Formed 1992 from The Queen's Regiment and The Royal Hampshire Regiment. Plate 21.
1st/2nd Battalion The Royal Regiment of Fusiliers. Reduced from three battalions in 1992. Plate 21.
1st/2nd Battalion The Royal Anglian Regiment. Reduced from three battalions in 1992. Plate 21.
1st Battalion The King's Own Royal Border Regiment. Plate 21.
1st Battalion The King's Regiment. Plate 20, fourth row.
1st Battalion The Prince of Wales's Own Regiment of Yorkshire. Plate 20, fourth row.

Cap badges.
Fig. 53. (Left)
The Royal
Regiment of
Fusiliers,
1968 to the
present.
Fig. 54.
(Right) Army
Air Corps,
1957 to the
present.

Cap badges. Fig. 55. (Left) Special Air Service Regiment, present day. Fig. 56. (Centre) Corps of Royal Electrical and Mechanical Engineers, 1947 to the present. Fig. 57. (Right) Royal Army Medical Corps, 1898 to the present.

1st Battalion The Green Howards. Fig. 15 and plate 20, fourth row.

1st Battalion The Queen's Lancashire Regiment. Plate 20.

1st Battalion The Duke of Wellington's Regiment. Fig. 22 and plate 20.

The Royal Irish Regiment. Formed in 1992 from The Royal Irish Rangers and The Ulster Defence Regiment. Badge: a crowned Irish harp. Plate 21.

1st Battalion The Devonshire and Dorset Regiment. Fig. 40 and plate 21.

1st Battalion The Cheshire Regiment. Fig. 16 and plate 21.

1st Battalion The Staffordshire Regiment. Plate 20, fifth row.

1st Battalion The Royal Welch Fusiliers. Plates 7, bottom row, but 'Welch' not 'Welsh', and 21.

1st Battalion The Royal Regiment of Wales. Plates 15, centre row (The Welsh Regiment), without scroll, and 21.

1st Battalion The Royal Gloucestershire, Berkshire and Wiltshire Regiment. Formed in 1994 from The Gloucestershire Regiment and The Duke of Edinburgh's Royal Regiment. Plate 20.

1st Battalion The Worcestershire and Sherwood Foresters Regiment. Plate 20, fifth row.

1st/2nd Battalions The Light Infantry. Reduced from three battalions in 1993. Plate 20, fifth row.

1st/2nd Battalions The Royal Green Jackets. Reduced from three battalions in 1992. Plate 20, fifth row.

1st Battalion The Royal Gurkha Rifles. Formed from 2nd King Edward VII's Own Gurkha Rifles and 6th Queen Elizabeth's Own Gurkha Rifles. Badge: crown surmounting crossed kukris. Plate 21.

2nd Battalion The Royal Gurkha Rifles. Formed from 7th Duke of Edinburgh's Own Gurkha Rifles and 10th Princess Mary's Own Gurkha Rifles. Badge: as 1st Battalion. Plate 21.

The Parachute Regiment. Plate 21, fifth row.

CORPS

Under 'Options for Change', certain corps were affected. In 1993 the corps of the British Army comprised the following:

The Royal Regiment of Artillery. Plate 20.

Royal Horse Artillery. Plate 20.

Corps of Royal Engineers (except Postal and Courier Services). Plate 20.

Royal Corps of Signals. Plate 20.

Army Air Corps. Fig. 54 and plate 20.

The Adjutant General's Corps. Plate 21. Formed in 1991 from: Women's Royal Army Corps (WRAC); Royal Army Pay Corps (RAPC); Royal Army Educational Corps (RAEC); Royal Military Police (RMP); Army Legal Corps (ALC); Staff Clerks of the Royal Army Ordnance Corps (RAOC); Royal Army Chaplains Department (RAChD); Military Provost Staff Corps (MPSC).

Royal Logistic Corps. Fig. 58 and plate 20. Formed in 1991 from: Royal Army Ordnance Corps (RAOC); Royal Corps of Transport (RCT); Royal Pioneer Corps (RPC); Army Catering Corps (ACC); Postal and Courier Services (RE).

Royal Army Medical Corps (RAMC). Fig. 57 and plate 21.

Corps of Royal Electrical and Mechanical Engineers (REME). Fig. 56 and plate 21.

Royal Army Veterinary Corps (RAVC). Plate 22a.

Small Arms School Corps. Plate 22a.

Royal Army Dental Corps (RADC). Plate 22a.

Intelligence Corps. Plate 22a.

Army Physical Training Corps. Plate 22a.

Queen Alexandra's Royal Army Nursing Corps. Plate 22a.

The Queen's Own Gurkha Engineers. Plate 21.

Queen's Gurkha Signals. Plate 21.

The Queen's Own Gurkha Transport Regiment. Plate 21.

General Service Corps. Plate 22a.

Fig. 58. The Royal Logistic Corps badge.

The British Army in the twenty-first century

In 2002 the British Army consisted of the following regiments and corps, listed with their full titles, which have now been finally agreed. The badges of all these, including corps variations, are shown in plates 20, 21 and 22a.

The Household Cavalry and Royal Armoured Corps

The Life Guards

The Blues and Royals (Royal Horse Guards and 1st Dragoons)

1st The Queen's Dragoon Guards

The Royal Scots Dragoon Guards
The Royal Dragoon Guards
The Queen's Royal Hussars (The Queen's Own and Royal Irish)
9th/12th Lancers (Prince of Wales's)
The King's Royal Hussars
The Light Dragoons
The Queen's Royal Lancers
The Royal Tank Regiment

The Foot Guards
1st Battalion Grenadier Guards
1st Battalion Coldstream Guards
1st Battalion Scots Guards
1st Battalion Irish Guards
1st Battalion Welsh Guards

The Infantry
The Royal Scots (The Royal Regiment)
The Royal Highland Fusiliers (Princess Margaret's Own Glasgow and Ayrshire Regiment)
The King's Own Scottish Borderers
The Black Watch (The Royal Highland Regiment)
The Highlanders (Seaforth, Gordon and Cameron)
The Argyll and Sutherland Highlanders (Princess Louise's)
The Princess of Wales's Royal Regiment (Queen's and Royal Hampshires)
The Royal Regiment of Fusiliers
The Royal Anglian Regiment
The King's Own Royal Border Regiment
The King's Regiment
The Prince of Wales's Own Regiment of Yorkshire
The Green Howards (Alexandra, Princess of Wales's Own Yorkshire Regiment)
The Queen's Lancashire Regiment
1st Battalion The Duke of Wellington's Regiment (West Riding)
The Royal Irish Regiment (27th [Inniskilling], 83rd, 87th and The Ulster Defence Regiment)
The Devonshire and Dorset Regiment
The Cheshire Regiment
1st Battalion The Royal Welch Fusiliers
1st Battalion The Royal Regiment of Wales
The Royal Gloucestershire, Berkshire and Wiltshire Regiment
The Worcestershire and Sherwood Foresters Regiment
The Staffordshire Regiment (The Prince of Wales's)
The Light Infantry
The Royal Green Jackets
The Royal Gurkha Rifles
The Queen's Gurkha Engineers
Queen's Gurkha Signals
The Queen's Own Gurkha Transport Regiment
The Parachute Regiment
Special Air Service Regiment

The rest of the Army
Royal Horse Artillery
The Royal Regiment of Artillery
Corps of Royal Engineers
Royal Corps of Signals
Army Air Corps
Royal Army Chaplain's Department
Royal Logistic Corps
Royal Army Medical Corps
Corps of Royal Electrical and Mechanical Engineers
The Adjutant General's Corps (SPS and ETS Branches)
The Adjutant General's Corps (Provost Branch – RMP) – Royal Military Police
The Adjutant General's Corps (Provost Branch – MPS) – Military Prison
  Service
The Adjutant General's Corps (ALS Branch) – Army Legal Service
Royal Army Veterinary Corps
Royal Army Dental Corps
Intelligence Corps
Army Physical Training Corps
General Service Corps
Queen Alexandra's Royal Army Nursing Corps

5. Care, display and identification

Care and cleaning

With a collection of badges and buttons, there are none of the major problems with care that beset collectors of other forms of militaria. There is no rust, the enemy of the weapon collector, nor are moths, except with embroidered and cloth badges, a cause of trouble as they are to the uniform collector. Badges and buttons, because of the very nature of the metals they are made of, require only careful cleaning when originally purchased and then casual maintenance thereafter. Because of the large numbers of badges and buttons about, only perfect, clear and unrubbed examples should be bought, except when an item is very old or rare. Repair of badges and buttons is not usually attempted because of the numbers available, but to an old or rare example this may be done, although some collectors prefer only to clean a rare damaged example.

One major enemy of badges and buttons, as with any metal, is abrasion. Badges and buttons should not be rubbed and rubbed to a brilliant shine, as would be expected by a sergeant-major, because this blurs the design and reduces the value. As long as the item is clean, this is sufficient. For silver items, the liquid products, in which the act of immersion cleans, are good, but this process too attacks the surface and should not be done more than necessary.

Larger badges and helmet plates should be dismounted if possible. This is best done with a good pair of long-nosed pliers with which to withdraw the metal pins holding the components together. These pins should be kept and replaced when the pieces have been cleaned. Make sure that all traces of metal polish are removed, as when dry this leaves a white film that is unsightly. Gilt items can be cleaned with ammonia solution, carefully applied with cotton wool and removed with warm water. If this is done with closed-back buttons, care must be taken that no deposits of water remain inside. If water has penetrated the back, it is best to leave the button in an airing cupboard, on a piece of paper on top of a radiator, or in a warm oven.

One word of warning concerning the repair of buttons: do not try to solder or braze on a new shank to a closed-back button, as the heat generated can cause the back to blow off with some force, which could cause injury. Also, do not apply heat to any metal inlaid with enamel, as this would be destroyed. If a badge is repaired by soldering or brazing, it will have to be carefully cleaned afterwards as the heat will discolour the metal.

Display of badges and buttons

The best way to display badges and buttons is on cards with a suitable background material. Small holes are made and the item is held in place with pins or matchsticks. These cards can then be stored in drawers or box files, with a suitable layer of tissue paper or felt between each. Once a complete set of a particular regiment or type has been accumulated, the cards could be framed and hung on the wall.

Another material most helpful in display is expanded polystyrene, into which the badge or button shanks can be gently pushed. Permanent displays are not advisable as one's collection will be constantly expanding.

Identification

The hardest part of all collecting is the identification of an item. This book describes many badges and buttons and illustrates varieties and types of each, but no book yet written has the answer to all identification problems. There are various basic questions one should ask oneself when setting out to identify an item. These questions will fill in much of the background and narrow the field of search.

1. Where was the item intended to be worn: head-dress plate, belt plate, cap badge, collar badge, pouch or sabretache badge?
2. What is the period? This can be determined from the crown: Georgian crown (plates 8, 9); Victorian crown (plate 8); Gwelphic crown (plate 12); Tudor crown (plate 11) – worn on items of Edward VII, George V, Edward VIII and George VI; Queen's crown (EIIR) (plate 21); or from the coat of arms: Hanoverian 1801–16 (fig. 5); 1816–37 (fig. 5); or Victorian and after (plate 10), as on the Royal Artillery plate.
3. For infantry. Is it before or after territorial titles (1881)?
4. For cavalry. Is it before or after the 1922 amalgamations? This can often be determined by the inclusion of two numbers or titles on the badge.

Once the above have been answered, the field is narrowed. It remains only to identify the regiment or unit and date. This is the hardest part, as variations abound – in cap badges more perhaps than in full-dress head-dress badges.

For buttons the questions are similar.

1. What is the metal? Bronze or pewter indicates that the button is before 1855. Gilt or silver buttons could be before or after then.
2. Is it before or after territorial titles (1881)?
3. If the button is numbered, check the list in this book. If it does not coincide, it *may* be an East India Company army button.

Identification will involve a certain amount of detective work, and the study of regimental battle honours is a useful guide when trying to distinguish between British Army and East India Company Army regiments. Dating may be made easier if the maker has marked the item. Reference should be made to the makers' names and dates (see pages 85–6).

The importance of battle honours on buttons, belt plates and head-dress plates is illustrated by the button shown on the right of the top line in plate 23, which shows '3' within a Garter inscribed 'Buxar' and 'Guzerat', the whole within an open laurel wreath. At first this might be taken to be an officer's button of the 3rd Foot. The button is closed-back and gilt; both pieces of information tally with the 3rd Foot for about 1840. The list on page 62, however, details a different pattern. The honours are checked and found to have been awarded to the 3rd Bengal Native Infantry. The back is marked Hawkes, Mosley & Co, Piccadilly, London. This is checked on page 85 and found to be the name of the firm from 1821 to 1852. The button is therefore an officer's button of the 3rd Bengal Native Infantry (which mutinied in 1857) of the period 1840–52.

6. Bibliography

Alderson, G.L.D. *Cap Badges of the British Army 1939–1945. Volume 1: Infantry. Volume 2: Armour, Artillery, Other Arms and Corps.* Author, 1989, 1990, 1998.

Badges and Their Meaning. G. Phillips & Sons, 1918.

Brereton, J.M. *A Guide to the Regiments and Corps of the British Army.* The Bodley Head, 1985.

Carman, W.Y. *Glengarry Badges of the British Army to 1881.* Arms and Armour Press, 1973.

Carman, W.Y. *Head Dresses of the British Army Cavalry.* Author, 1968.

Chichester, H.M., and Burgess-Short, G. *Records and Badges of the British Army.* Gale & Polden, 1900; reprinted 1970.

Edwards, T.J. *Regimental Badges.* Gale & Polden, 1956.

Gaylor, John. *Military Badge Collecting.* Pen and Sword Books/Leo Cooper, 2000.

Gaylor, John. *The Regimental Cap Badge Collection.* Military Mailwise, 1990.

Kipling, A., and King, H. *Badges of the British Army. Volume 1: To the End of the Great War. Volume 2: End of the Great War to the Present.* F. Muller, 1978, 1979.

Parkyn, Major H.G. *Shoulder Belt Plates and Buttons.* Gale & Polden, 1956.

Ripley, Howard. *Buttons of the British Army.* Arms and Armour Press, 1983.

Taylor, Peter. *Collecting Anodised Cap Badges.* Pen and Sword Books/Leo Cooper, 1998.

Wilkinson, F. *Badges of the British Army 1820 to the Present Day.* Cassell Military, 1997.

Wilkinson-Latham, R. and C. *Home Service Helmet.* Star Products, 1970.

Dress Regulations for the Army: 1822, 1834, 1846, 1855, 1857, 1874, 1883, 1894, 1900, 1911 and 1934.

Journal of the Military Historical Society.

Journal of the Society of Army Research.

Military Illustrated.

Soldier magazine.

7. British badge and button makers

All addresses are in London except those marked (B) which are in Birmingham. Some of the London makers listed had works in Birmingham, but only their London address appeared on their wares.

Armfield
Edward Armfield, Newall Street (B), 1790–1890
Edward Armfield, St Paul's Square (B), 1891–1910
Edward Armfield & Co Ltd, St Paul's Square (B), 1911–1940

Army and Navy Company
Army and Navy Co-operative Society, 117 Victoria Street, 1873–1889
Army and Navy Co-operative Society, 105 Victoria Street, 1889–1934

Donler
William Donler, 42 Cherry Street (B), c.1870–1890

Firmin (established 1673)
Samuel Firmin, Strand opposite New Church, 1763–1768
Samuel Firmin, near Somerset House, 1769–1782
Firmin & Sons, 153 Strand, 1783–1796
Firmin & Westall, 1797–1811
Phillip Firmin, 1812–1814
Firmin & Langdale, 153 Strand and 10 Claire Court, 1815–1821
Firmin & Sons, 153 Strand and 10 Claire Court, 1822–1828
P. & R. Firmin, 153 Strand and White Horse Yard, 1829–1834
P. R. & S. Firmin, 153 Strand, 1835–1837
Samuel Firmin & Sons, 153 Strand, 1838
Firmin & Sons, 153 Strand, 1839
Phillip & Samuel Firmin, 153 Strand and 13 Conduit Street, 1839–1849
Phillip Firmin & Sons, 153 Strand and 13 Conduit Street, 1850–1854
P. V. Firmin & Sons, 153 Strand and 13 Conduit Street, 1855
Firmin & Sons, 153 Strand and 13 Conduit Street, 1856–1860
Firmin & Sons, 153–154 Strand and 13 Conduit Street, 1861–1863
Firmin & Sons, 153–155 Strand and 13 Conduit Street, 1864–1879
Firmin & Sons Ltd, 153–155 Strand and 47 Warwick Street, 1880–1894
Firmin & Sons Ltd, 108–109 St Martin's Lane and 47 Warwick Street, 1895–1904
Firmin & Sons Ltd, 108–109 St Martin's Lane and 6 Warwick Street, 1905–1915
Firmin & Sons Ltd, 8 Cork Street, 1916–1968
Firmin & Sons Ltd, Crawford Street, 1968–1972
Firmin and Sons Ltd, Globe Works, New Town Row (B), 1994
(Firmin now incorporates J. R. Gaunt and Smith & Wright.)

Gaunt
J. R. Gaunt and Sons Ltd, 1900–1994
J. R. Gaunt & Sons, London, –1982 (see Firmin). Also at Birmingham 1898–1994.

Harvey
Joseph Harvey, 16 Upper Priory (B), 1800–1803
Joseph Harvey, Park Street (B), 1815

Hawkes
Thomas Hawkes, 17 Piccadilly, 1788–1796
Thomas Hawkes, 24 Piccadilly, 1797–1809
T. Hawkes, Mosley & Co, 22 Piccadilly, 1810–1820
Hawkes, Mosley & Co, 14 Piccadilly, 1821–1852
Hawkes & Co, 14 Piccadilly, 1853–1890
Hawkes & Co Ltd, 1 Saville Row, 1891–1974
Gieves and Hawkes, 1 Saville Row, 1974 to date (acquired by Gieves, 1974)

Hobson
Hobson & Sons, 94 Great Windmill Street and 43–44 Artillery Place, Woolwich, 1873–1877
Hobson & Sons, 37–38 Little Windmill Street and Woolwich, 1878–1883

Hobson & Sons, 37–38 Little Windmill Street, 1884–1886
Hobson & Sons, 1–5 Lexington Street, 1887–1972
Hobson & Sons, 154 Tooley Street, 1994
Hobson & Sons, Lewisham, 2000

Jennens
Jennens and Co, 1800–1832
Charles Jennens, 1833–1912
Jennens & Co, London, 1912–1924
(After 1860, the Prince of Wales's feathers appeared on the back of buttons.)

Leonard
William Leonard & Co, Aston Street (B), 1803
Leonard & Co, Aston Street (B), 1815
William Leonard & Son, Aston Street (B), 1816–1820
Leonard & Son, Aston Street (B), 1821

Merry, Phipson and Parker
Merry, Phipson and Parker, Cherry Street (B), 1830–1870

Nutting
I. Nutting, Covent Garden, 1800–1840
(Nutting made most of the pewter other ranks' buttons.)

Pitt
Charles Pitt & Co, 50 St Martin's Lane, 1875–1895
Charles Pitt & Co, 31 Maddox Street, 1896

Reeves
Charles Reeves, 8 Aire Street, Piccadilly, 1853–1863
Charles Reeves, 18 St Martin's Street, 1902–1909
Charles Reeves, 9 West Street, Golden Square, 1910–1937
Charles Reeves, 9 Newburgh Street, 1938–1955

Sherlock
Thomas Sherlock, 15 King Street, Covent Garden, 1837–1846
Sherlock & Company, 15 King Street, Covent Garden, 1847–1887

Starkey
J. Starkey & Co, 1 Spur Street, Leicester Square, 1835–1836
Joseph Starkey or Josh Starkey, 3 Old Bond Street, 1837–1855
Joseph Starkey, 23 Conduit Street, 1856–1914
Joseph Starkey, 45 Conduit Street, 1915–1918
Joseph Starkey, 21 George Street, Hanover Square, 1919–1934
(and at other addresses up to the present day)

Thompson
William Thompson, 11 Air Street, Piccadilly, 1820s

Toye, Kenning & Spencer
Toye, Kenning & Spencer Ltd, 19–21 Great Queen Street, WC2

*The list of other makers below has been gleaned from buttons and badges. The dates given
are those of the items from which the name was noted.*
Buttons Ltd; also marked as Buttons Limited, with either 'Birmingham' or crossed swords
    trademark
Cook & Palmer, Woolwich; 1890s
Harman & Co, Calcutta, India
Will Harris, Birmingham; noted on pewter buttons
I. McGowan; noted on silver buttons, c.1810, and pewter buttons
Mills & Co, London; noted on pewter buttons
Player Bros, Birmingham; c.1880
Ranken & Co, London and India; established 1770
Reynolds, London; also J. W. Reynolds & Co, 30 St Martin's Lane; 1880 onward
Smith & Wright, Birmingham; makers of the other ranks' buttons from 1855 (now part of
    Firmin & Sons Ltd)
W. Twigg & Co Ltd, London, c.1840
H. Watson, King Street, Covent Garden

Index